Praise for *Guitar Highway Rose*

'The book is a great insight into people and the way they feel and think – a charming medley of characters' thoughts, words, feelings, actions, reactions, hopes and dreams.' *Viewpoint*

'Lowry's deft and daring style is a heady mix of genres and points of view which are never the less woven into a seamless whole … a thoroughly enjoyable book.' *Magpies*

'Lowry's prose is crisply observant in some places, stream-of-consciousness in others, and full of humour and one-liners … a romantic, entertaining and thoughtful novel.' *School Library Journal*, USA

Guitar Highway Rose was shortlisted for the 1998 Children's Book Council of Australia's Book of the Year Award for older readers, the 1998 Victorian Premier's Literary Awards, and the 1997 Western Australian Premier's Book Awards. It was Highly Commended in the 1998 Family Award for Children's Literature, and was the Winner of the 1999 Hoffman Award in the West Australian Young Reader's Book Awards (nominated and voted by young readers).

Praise for *With Lots of Love from Georgia*

'An honest, entertaining and affectionate account of one girl's journey through a year of adolescence. *Kids into Books*, NZ

'Lowry … seems to have a direct line into the minds and feelings of teenagers' Australian Centre for Youth Literature

With Lots of Love from Georgia was the Winner of the 2006 New Zealand Post Young Adult Book Award and was shortlisted for both the Western Australian Premier's Young Adult Book Award and the LIANZA Esther Glen Award.

juicy writing

inspiration and techniques for young writers

Brigid Lowry

ALLEN&UNWIN

First published in 2008

Allen & Unwin
83 Alexander St
Crows Nest NSW 2065
Australia
Phone: (61 2) 8425 0100
Fax: (61 2) 9906 2218
Email: info@allenandunwin.com
Web: www.allenandunwin.com

National Library of Australia
Cataloguing-in-Publication entry:

Lowry, Brigid.
Juicy writing.

ISBN 978 174175 048 5.

1. Authorship – Juvenile literature.
2. Creative writing (Secondary education). I. Title.

808.02

Cover design by Beci Orpin Studios
Text design by Sandra Nobes
Set in Minion by Tou-Can Design
Printed in Australia by McPherson's Printing Group

10 9 8 7 6 5 4

Brigid Lowry was born in New Zealand and has returned to live there after many years in Australia. After the success of *Guitar Highway Rose*, she wrote *Follow the Blue*, and then she collaborated with her son, Sam Field, on the fantasy adventure *Space Camp*. Brigid's next novel, *With Lots of Love from Georgia*, won the Young Adult Section of the New Zealand Children's Post Book Awards in 2006. Her latest book, *Tomorrow All Will Be Beautiful*, is a wonderful collection of her stories and poetry.

Brigid teaches creative writing and also writes poetry and fiction for adults. She is in favour of op shops, travel, nectarines, coloured pencils and rivers.

Dedicated to my late parents,
Bob and Irene,
who gave me inky fingers.

An Invitation

Writing is a joyous act. It's a pleasurable journey into the world of the imagination and the world of ideas. It brings our deep loves and our sorrows into the light and transforms them, connecting us not only to ourselves but to other human beings. Good writing begins in the heart, with honesty and interesting thoughts, and takes us to places we didn't know we were capable of going.

Good writing produces work that is profound, whether it be a song, a poem, a play, a short story, a novel or a film script. Words are important and our stories matter.

There are many books for writers. In the eighteen years since I've been writing professionally, I've read quite a few of them. Some have inspired and encouraged me, others have given me solid technical help. This book aims to do both. It's written for, but not restricted to, young writers, and is a distillation of information that's been beneficial to my own writing life. It is also fed by my years as a Zen student, a creative writing teacher, and an avid collector of wisdom from other writers.

This book contains an invitation to you, the writer. It invites you to embark on a long mysterious journey for which there is no real map. However, in these pages you'll find guidance and companionship. You don't need anything you don't already have: courage, a willing spirit and an enquiring mind. Here, every part of you is welcome: your longings, your heartbreak, your flimsy dreams, your unique intelligence. Come on in.

Brigid Lowry

Contents

hello

ONE
STARTING OUT

Sunflowers and seeds

Where does writing come from? It comes from our depths, in its own time and its own inexplicable way, almost as if by magic. However, if you love the world of words, there are things you can do to encourage the writing process. The first step is to collect material.

In this way, writing is a bit like gardening. You begin by making compost. Gardeners collect leaves, food scraps, lawn clippings and seaweed, but your raw material is words and ideas. Scribble a line in your notebook. Let it rest for a while. It may be a word that you love, an image, or an idea for a story. Honour the deep murky ocean of your imagination. Let the material accumulate, however slight or random it may seem. This process requires trust. You don't have to know how these fragments are going to be used, just write them down. Your job is to collect things that interest you, and to believe that they are worth collecting. Allow this compost, or seed material, to gather in dark ungainly confusion.

Later, when the time is right, and you're in the mood to write, take out your notebook and play. Take a line and add another. Follow an idea and see where it leads you. Explore possibilities. You will begin to see connections between some of the stuff you have gathered. Maybe the guy in the black fedora hat you saw in a café, the one who drank two lattes in a row and didn't wipe the froth off his lip, owns the talking dog you jotted down when it appeared in your bizarre dream. The scribbled words 'talking dog?' suddenly interest you again. 'On the day Fifi, the talking poodle, was run over…' you begin. You feel a sudden rush of interest and pleasure as your brain kicks into action and something begins to take shape. Like gardening, writing is a hit and miss process. Certain seeds will germinate, others won't. Sometimes, however hard you try, that good line will refuse to build into anything larger. Never mind. Leave it alone. Let it return to the dark soil of your subconscious. Other seed material will miraculously take root and develop into something wonderful. Line by line, a poem sprouts. A fragment transforms into a short story. A song blossoms into an opera. The joy comes with surrendering to and trusting the process. As in a garden, delight comes with the mystery.

Exercises

* Invent a new garden implement. What materials is it made from? What is its function?

* What would your dream garden be like?

* If you lived in a garden, what would you be? A bluebird? A witty garden gnome? An echidna? A broken mosaic

birdbath? The bag lady in the shed, who is possibly a witch?

❧ Many odd things are buried in gardens. Write a story that involves digging. Beware of clichés. If there is a dead body in your story, you'll have to make sure you're not rehashing a stale plot stolen from a TV show.

❧ Write an 'Intense Tale of Exile' involving bittersweet love, war, bravery, sacrifice and betrayal. Set it in the world of SNAILS.

❧ Two unlikely characters meet in a garden. A girl in a wheelchair? A waitress? A wizard? Something happens during their meeting that changes them both. Tell their story in five hundred words. Make use of sensory detail, because gardens are alive with sounds, smells, textures. Give your piece a fabulous title.

Starters

⟜ When I lived in a tree house…

⟜ You will run through a patch of wild flowers screaming…

⟜ When I was six I made friends with a pixie…

⟜ Radioactive chives…

⟜ At night the wind sounded like a mad dog barking…

⟜ Fred enjoyed potatoes but…

↬ Ophelia and Bedelia are making daisy chains…

↬ I remember mud and rotten pumpkins…

↬ She sat under the striped sun umbrella drinking….

↬ Bare feet are good

↬ My grandfather did not believe in flowers…

↬ There will be a circus in the garden shed at 3pm…

↬ A box of secrets lies buried…

↬ Certain things made the worm grumpy

↬ King Turnip and Madame Pumpkin

↬ In soft rain…

↬ A man needs a shed. Actually, so does a woman. However, only some fifteen year olds need a shed.

↬ As the spade said to the trowel…

↬ Edible flowers

↬ It takes a long time to cut a lawn with nail scissors

↬ Hindsight is a wonderful thing. Looking back, it seems obvious that my mother shouldn't have made my eighth birthday celebration a garden party.

Good ideas and how to get them

Writing is not hard. Just get paper and pencil, sit down and write it as it occurs to you. The writing is easy – it's the occurring that's hard. Stephen Leacock

It's been said that if you've survived childhood you already have enough material for a lifetime of writing. One of the questions that people often ask writers is where they get their ideas. The answer is simple. Your everyday life is abundant with ideas, if you have the ability to notice them.

Muriel Rukeyser said that the world is made of stories. It's also made of rabbits and roses, sunsets and sadness, lizards and longings. It contains everything: soup, itchy scarves, Japanese hip hop, raspberry smoothies, old suitcases, dodgy deals and slippery slopes. Your job as a writer is to stay alive to all of it, to collect the world and turn it into stories.

It doesn't have to be something of epic proportions to be good material. Even a small thing becomes important, if it is told well. The following poem, by Perth poet and musician, Ross Bolleter, is a great example of taking something ordinary and turning it into poetry.

> Washing at night
> Slinging it up cold and heavy
>> Wet under the misted stars
>
> Morning each black T shirt's hung
>> With powdered galaxies of
> Oh God one ancient Kleenex

If you are awake to it, your own life will provide endless good material for your writing. For example, you have a soul-destroying fight with your sister. It feels like the end of the world, but it isn't. Two weeks later you're best friends again. She even lends you her MP3 player, which is very cool. Even better, because you are a writer, nothing need be wasted. The short story you're working on for the school magazine needs conflict. Use the insults you fired at your sister and give them to one of your characters. Using the material of your own life in your fiction in such a way will give your work the ring of truth.

Feeling short of ideas?

Here are some places you might find inspiration.

In the newspaper. The world is a mysterious place. As the old saying goes, there's nothing so weird as folks. Newspapers and magazines are full of AMAZING TRUE STORIES. For example: Did you know that the first bomb dropped by the Allies during World War II killed the elephant at the Berlin zoo? Or that a tiger has striped skin as well as striped fur? Somehow, for me, those two odd facts that I found in a newspaper quiz seem to go together. My mind begins to imagine a zoo, and a mood. This moment of recognition is almost not rational. It is the flimsy cobwebby possibility of a beginning of something. For a writer, that moment of interest is important. It contains the germ of something significant enough to be scribbled down and thought about, a seed idea which later may find its way into a poem, a story or a scene in a novel. The family who are aiming to get into the *Guinness Book of Records* by building the world's largest wall of sausages. A young couple who were prepared to sell the rights to their unborn child's name to a corporation for a million dollars. For me oddities such as these, discovered in my newspaper, inspire many possibilities. I can feel a story coming on. 'Once upon a time there was a kid named Coca Cola…'

So, when you're having an imagination drought, get on down to your local library and spend some time browsing in the newspapers. International ones such as *The Hong Kong Times* can be particularly fascinating. Take your notebook, because there are luscious ideas just waiting to be picked.

Poetry books and songs are often a stimulating source of good beginnings for a piece of writing. Take a line that intrigues you and let it lead you towards a poem or a song of your own.

Cemeteries are full of stories. Wander around on a sunny afternoon reading the headstones, then let your imagination take flight. The young man struck by lightning, aged 17 years, November 27th, 1902. Who was he? Was he a farm labourer or the rich son of landed gentry? Where was he going on the day he was killed? Was anyone secretly relieved that he died? His sister might have been, if he were arrogant and cruel and it meant she'd inherit the farm. Keep on asking the question *What If?* Follow the story and see where it takes you. Let the mossy graves provide tendrils of ideas. Write them down. Take them further.

Step outside your comfort zone and go to a place you've never been. A bridal shop, a posh café, the railway station, anywhere that's not your usual sort of haunt. Then use it to inspire some writing. TWO PAGES, make it brilliant!

Starters

Lists of starters are fun. You can compile your own, maybe using some of those good lines from your juicy writing notebook. You can make them up as a game with friends or family. When you feel like writing, take out your list of starters, pick one that intrigues you and go for it. Or try the following:

Write about:

* When robots go bad
* Slime balls
* The day after I died
* The world's most boring job
* When the lampshade fell in love with the light bulb
* Why I am scared of fairies
* Op shops
* It was a queer time
* It started with bananas on toast for breakfast...
* Evil flowers
* Purple pens
* Strange habits
* Being four
* Being fabulous
* I told her my name was Daisy
* Sipping sunflowers on lazy days
* Glossy bossy people
* Travels with my aunt
* The day things started disappearing

Creative spaces

Having a creative space is really important if you are to be a writer. It's possible to write anywhere, and many fine ideas have been scribbled down on the back of an envelope while in a crowded café, or jotted down in a notebook when sitting on a bus. However, if writing is important to you, it's important to dedicate a space to it. Creating an area and dedicating it to writing is a way of honouring your creativity and inviting the muse to come on in.

If you're lucky enough to have your own room, and a desk, that's terrific. There's no such thing as the housework police, but personally I find that mess and clutter crowd my mind as well as my physical space, so I suggest getting rid of anything that is no longer functional or precious to you. Toss out dead pens, old papers and books you'll never read again. Take the books to the local op shop and make some free good karma while you're at it. Of course, some people work best in chaos, so if that applies to you, your room will contain all sorts of weird stuff, spread everywhere, and who am I to say a thing against it?

Funking it up. If your creative space is incomplete, or feels less than creative, make a wish list. Scrounge up a desk or an old table. Paint it or drape a cloth on it. Make a bookshelf out of bricks and a plank. Surround yourself with objects that are meaningful to you. Maybe it's a postcard of Chinese acrobats, or the bleached skull of a dead bird. My son Sam, a twenty-something documentary film-maker, has figurines of Tin Tin and Snowy. I've got a collection of heart-shaped rocks and a plastic pineapple. The heart rocks remind me to love my life, the pineapple symbolises the spirit of play.

Honour your creativity by creating a real live space for it and furnishing it with the things you love. Whatever your age, you're always the right age to have fun. Surround yourself with a paint box, index cards, any good stuff that takes your fancy. Fragrance can be an added bonus. Choose incense or candles to enhance your mood. Is it a vanilla morning, a rose night, a musky sandalwood afternoon?

Some people work best in quiet, other people like music. Experiment with what works best for you. It's good not to have a hard and fast rule. Some days sinking into the quiet may be required, other times some melancholy jazz or sweet hip-hop will be the perfect choice.

Claim your space. If you have a hugely noisy family and share a room with your brothers and sisters it's a bit more of a challenge, but it's still important to claim some creative space. It might be an old armchair on the verandah where you sit with your breakfast and your MP3 player. It might be a sunny spot in the library on the way home from school with your travelling tools: a purple pen and an old exercise book. Whatever your circumstances, make it your quest to find a place, or places, where you can truly relax and write.

Dunedin artist Kerry McKay is the queen of creative spaces. The art room at the College of Education where she works is bright with Mexican paper friezes, colourful paintings and quirky sculptures. When I was doing a writing residency at the college, I was finding it hard to work in a grey room in a grey office building known as The Tower. It was winter, I was homesick, I'd lost my sparkle. So Kerry decorated a big brown paper bag with bright colours for me. She sketched a lively Poetry Girl on it, and wrote the words Collect Ideas. I hung it on my wall nearby. It cheered me up, gave me permission to frolic and play, and helped my writing flow again.

Kerry's also the duchess of creative bags. When I left Dunedin she made me a beautiful gift that I will always treasure. It's a small old-fashioned suitcase with one of my poems written inside. It is a tribute to creativity with its tartan fabric lining, tartan ribbon bow, and spooky tail of fake hair from the $2 shop hanging from the lid. Three pictures are glued inside: a cherry tart, a tin and a girl, making the slogan: Tartan Girl. How fabulous!

So you see, even a suitcase, a fishing tackle box, or a basket can become a creative space – a place to store pens, pencils, paper, toys, special rocks or shells. Many writers use a corkboard or a whiteboard to display quotes, postcards, images, ideas that interest and inspire them.

What else will you need in your creative space?
A computer is good but not essential. A dictionary.
A thesaurus. A library of books that you love. A collection
of stationery: paper, pens, pencils, coloured pencils,
highlighters, textas, glue and scissors, stapler.

You will also need a sense of humour, plenty of patience,
a willingness to go beyond your comfort zone, and what
Bryce Courtney refers to as bum glue: the ability to sit glued
to your chair for hours while the work gets done.

Good quotes for creative spaces:

*The place where memory meets imagination in
the dark.*　　　　　　　　　　　　　　　Jack Kerouac

*Easy is right. Begin right and you are easy. Continue
easy and you are right.*　　　　　　　　　Chuang-Tsu

How do I work? I grope.　　　　　　　Albert Einstein

Stay light on your feet and risk delight.
　　　　　　　　　　　　　　　　George Alexander, artist

*I met, not long ago, a young man who aspired to become
a novelist. Knowing that I was in the profession, he asked
me to tell him how he should set to work to realize his
ambition. I did my best to explain. 'The first thing,' I
said, 'is to buy quite a lot of paper, a bottle of ink, and a
pen. After that you merely have to write.'*　　Aldous Huxley

Notebooks and journals

I have a host of notebooks. There's one in my bag for jottings and thoughts that arrive at inconvenient times. I have a dream journal by my bed, for recording and working with dreams. On my desk there's an encouragement journal in which I save all the encouraging things that friends say or write to me. I also use a visual diary, and I have a daily journal. Other creative people have one huge journal that serves all of the above purposes and beyond. Big journals are a record of a life, and can contain love letters, feathers, photographs, quotes, bus tickets, poems, words, anything you like.

Let's start with the basics. Get a notebook.

You don't have to spend heaps. I often buy a cheap school exercise book for less than a dollar, then frisk it up by pasting a picture or a wild collage on the cover. My most recent purchase looks superb covered in green and gold psychedelic contact paper. Feel free to splash out on an expensive one with a suede cover if it makes you happy.

Right, so now you have a notebook. Cool. Carry it everywhere. Use it to jot down good words, phrases, ideas. Tune in to interesting conversations, make a note of lines of dialogue that intrigue you.

- 'Never marry a man with a bad back,' the silvery blonde woman in a café tells her buxom friend.

- 'I think too much and I talk too much,' the skinny guy with the Celtic tattoo says loudly to his girlfriend, as you pass them in the street.

- 'We had to write about the lady who loved cherries,' you hear a kid say to his mum.

Write it down. These lines in your notebook are valuable. They provide a treasure trove of material that will be useful, even if at first you're not sure how. Novelist Richard Ford collects everything he can: dreams, random images, lines and snippets, things he overhears, items he reads in the paper. He records them all in his notebook, and when he has enough of them, his characters begin to emerge.

Sometimes an interesting line appears all by itself, out of the depths of your imagination, like a gift. 'Once I was mad and lived on the edge of nowhere,' is a line that came to me as I sat waiting for a train, gazing aimlessly at the vivid blue of the Indian Ocean. It seemed like a worthwhile line so I jotted it down, though I had no particular use for it. Some months later, hearing of a radio competition requiring short stories of 750 words, I got out my line, and began a story, which won a prize.

'How to mend a Broken Heart'

Once I was mad and lived on the edge of
nowhere, planting basil and bright nasturtiums,
slowly dreaming the days away and folding myself
into the corners of the night, folding time into
squares of old newspaper and cutting the squares
into stars and hearts and rows of paper dolls.
I slept by myself under a blue quilt and ate bread
and cheese dipped in soup from a Chinese bowl.
I loved a man who didn't love me. It was an old
story and a sad story and nobody cared a fig.
Or maybe they did.

(If you'd like to read the whole story you can find it in
Tomorrow All Will Be Beautiful.)

Yay for the notebook! Many writers also keep a
daily journal or diary. There are many reasons for this.
It's a good way of staying in touch with yourself and your
feelings. It can bring clarity and focus at the end of a long
hard day. It is a safe place to be yourself, when the world
seems murky. The mere act of putting black on white keeps
the writing muscle going.

Keeping a daily journal also feeds your work in ways
that are not always known to you. One brilliant example
of this happened to poet Audre Lourde, who had a period
in her life when everything turned to custard. Just about
everything that could go wrong went very wrong and
Lourde felt completely overwhelmed and exhausted.

During this time she wrote furiously in her journal. What she wrote seemed to her to be self-indulgent and scrambled, but it also felt like her lifeline to sanity. One of her great despairs during that time was that she was unable to write any poetry. However, some time later, Lourde reread her feverishly scratched journals and was amazed to discover a series of strong poems.

A visual diary. Every evening I get out my hard-backed drawing book, in which each large page is divided into eight squares, and I draw a picture. I use one of the little squares daily. Other people might choose to use a whole page, but I like doing a small picture. Whatever I draw means something to me that day. It might be a wild angry scribble in red and orange, it might be a small blue cloud with the word *sleepy* written in it. I always feel grounded and creative when I take the time to use my coloured pencils and draw my day. Don't limit yourself to only one art form. Collage, painting, photography are all great ways to explore creativity.

 Experiment with journals. Journaling is a fantastic tool. Again, there are no limits. Use a small notebook one time, a classy fabulous journal the next time. Many writers do it all on their laptop. Others prefer pen on paper. Experiment with whatever works best for you. Start a dream journal, a collection of story ideas, a collection of good words, a scrapbook of visual stimuli that appeal to you, or a diary of a year.

TWO

TRANSFORMING YOUR WORLD

The most fascinating person in the world: Me!

The reason I write is that you can travel and be whoever you want without even getting off your ass. I guess that's why I do it so much. francesca wilkins, age 15

Our writing comes from who we are. Every single thing we've ever seen, felt, heard, known or tasted lives inside of us. Some of it's conscious, some is half-remembered, shadowy as a dream, while some is buried deep and waiting to be rediscovered. This fertile maelstrom provides material that is ours to shape into fiction. Every writer has an entire history of people and places and events to call upon and use, however they wish to. Some like to write autobiography, others like to fictionalise their material, and others combine those two strategies. Many first novels, both successful and unsuccessful ones, are closely based on the author's own life. *Prep* by Curtis Sittenfield, and *Oranges are not the Only Fruit* by Jeanette Winterson, are examples of writers who use the story of their own life as the basis for a book.

In order to be a writer, you have to know yourself well. The process of self-discovery is ongoing, because the person you are today is not the person you'll be next Friday, let alone next year. Things happen and life changes you. If you're sincere about taking writing as your path, you must be prepared to continue to explore the question of who you are and your relationship to the world. Because if you stay on the surface, if you're content to coast, then your work will reflect this shallowness. Who are you?

Getting to know yourself: a Quiz

* Are you an optimist or a pessimist?

* How old are you really? Forget your biological age. Are you a playful 7 year old? Are you a 307 year old who comes from another planet?

* What is your biggest fear?

* What is your smallest fear?

* What things do you know something about? (Computers? Horses? Mermaids? Cooking? Fishing?)

* What are ten things you'd like to do before you die?

* Ten things you want to do before Christmas?

* Ten things you want for Christmas that don't cost any money?

* Ten things you think the planet could do without?

* List four things you're not in the least bit interested in, that your parents want you to be interested in.

- If you were an object of clothing, what would you be?

- If you were a kitchen appliance, what would you be?

- What is your favourite colour? Why? Write a piece about it.

Here's one I wrote about yellow:

I am egg, bud, skirt, sunflower. I am butter, waxy, salty and delicious. I'm a child's hair, pale as the silk on sweet corn. Once I was dark, but now yellow suffuses my world with saffron light. It is the sun colour, it is the moon colour; it sounds like a bell and tastes of honey. Yellow dreams fill my moon nights, glowing gold as a witch's petticoat, mysterious as turmeric, delicate as dust.

Exercises

Michael Kimball is a novelist who uses the material of his life to craft strong fiction. He writes about his grandmother's death in his novel *How Much of Us There Was*.

Kimball says he uses the material of his own life because for him 'The family is a strong context for writing about difficult and meaningful subjects – loss, grief, need, and also love.' He says that the family matters to all of us in one way or another and that he's 'trying to write novels that somehow matter.'

Write a page about your family. Let the things that matter to you about them be truthfully told on the page.

'You have to tell me a story' said Poppy to her father, 'before you go to work.' 'I can't, and you know why. I don't know any stories any more.' 'Yes you do. Stories from your life. Just make something up, like you used to. It's easy. You just say, Once upon a time, and then say whatever comes into your head.'

Helen Garner, from *The Children's Bach*

One of the best things about writing is that in a sense, you get to play God. You can mix and match, by taking things that really happened and layering them with things that could have, should have, or might have happened.

Take something from your life and extend it. Allow it to lead you somewhere really interesting. Start with the magical phrase *Once upon a time...* and let your imagination carry you anywhere it wants to go.

Dirty knees exercise. I recently fell in love with a great line from a prose piece called 'Final Fantasy' by Sheila Heti.

When I'm twenty five I'll wash the dirt off my knees.

Write a piece based on her line, beginning with the age you will turn on your next birthday. Begin each line with the words 'When I'm...' and keep going until you reach twenty-five. If you are already twenty-five, start wherever you are. Or pick any years you like. Make the work your own and have fun!

Here is my friend Grace Goodfellow's version.

When I'm sixteen, I'll wash the dirt off my
  knees.
When I'm seventeen, I'll pull a face at myself
  in the mirror and giggle.
When I'm eighteen, I'll drive around Australia
  — fruit picking, singing and smiling.
When I'm nineteen, I'll meet a delightful uni
  boy and fall madly in love with him.
When I'm twenty, I'll sing karaoke in a bar
  with my best friend.
When I'm twenty-one, I'll tell everyone I
  can't believe how old I'm getting!
When I'm twenty-two, I'll learn to like
  coffee.
When I'm twenty-three, I'll complain about
  my next birthday.
When I'm twenty-four, I'll run into the uni
  student I once loved and we'll have lunch by
  a quiet river together.
When I'm twenty-five, I'll be half way to
  fifty. And I'll be happy.

In 2007 Grace won a writing competition that was held as
part of the Somerset Celebration of Literature, where she
met another fabulous young winning writer, Josephine de
Costa. Here's Josie's version. You might need your hankie,
because this is a powerful and sad piece.

When I'm sixteen, I won't think about poetry
    when I should be doing chemistry homework
    (there is no beauty in the fact that Al +
    O₂ = Al₂O₃).

When I'm seventeen, the world will be a
    little closer to the sun.

When I'm eighteen, maybe the world will look
    different from outer space.

When I'm nineteen, maybe they will have
    cleaned out your room.

When I'm twenty, I'll be out of here, but
    you'll never be able to move now.

When I'm twenty-one, I'll have a cake and
    maybe someone will give me a key.

When I'm twenty-two, I'll probably throw the
    key away.

When I'm twenty-three, your parents might
    be able to think about you without hurting.

When I'm twenty-four, I probably won't think
    about you much anymore.

When I'm twenty-five, I'll wash the dirt off
    my knees,

But you can't ever wash yours.

For Jenna. (Jenna was my friend in junior
school, but we kind of grew apart. I hadn't
seen her for six months. She committed suicide
on Tuesday night.)

Some people walk in the rain, others just get wet.

Roger Miller, musician

If you want to be a writer, you have to become a person who walks in the rain. You have to be able to take ordinary life and make it extraordinary, with the powerful magic wand of pen and ink.

Take an incident that has happened to you recently and transform it into something splendid. It can be as simple as watching people in the mall, or helping a kid fix their skateboard, but if you tell it right, it will be juicy writing.

Daily free writing

Here are the writing instructions that Jaya was given in 'Petalheads', a story in *Tomorrow All Will Be Beautiful*.

> *Write about you. Go for ten minutes. Write whatever comes into your mind. Don't think too hard.*
> *Just go for it.*

This seemingly simple writing exercise is one you could do every day of your life. Every single time you did it you'd discover new treasures. By giving yourself the daily freedom to be, write, think and say whatever you want, your writing will really improve.

What informs you?

Let us face a pluralistic world in which there are no universal churches, no single remedy for all diseases, no one way to teach or write or sing, no magic diet, no world poets, and no chosen races, but only the wretched and wonderfully diversified human race.

Jacques Barzun

The simplest questions are the most profound. Where were you born? Where is your home? Where are you going? What are you doing? Think about these once in a while and watch your answers change.

Richard Bach, writer

Each one of us is a unique human being. No one before, during or after our lifetime will ever be quite the same as us. We often take our own life and our individuality for granted, partly because we are deep in it, and also because we know it so well. Writers often worry that their stories are not very interesting, because they are so used to being themselves and their world feels so familiar that it can also seem unworthy.

Most of us do not know our own beauty. We see and admire the fine qualities of others, but are blind to our own attributes. This is often demonstrated in a writing class. Each writer happily responds to a given topic and feels satisfied with what they've written, until it comes time to read their work aloud. At this point it's common to lose heart, because all the other work shines so brightly. The first person reads and their sentences are impressively elegant. The next reads, and although their work is not as polished, it is abundant with original ideas. Suddenly it's your turn. Fear sets in. Your piece of writing, which was fine a minute ago, now feels so lame that you don't want anyone to hear it. Yet actually, although you can't see it, yours has something special too. Perhaps a delicious wit or some strong ideas, which are dazzling in their own unique way.

Trusting that you have your own voice, and that it is valid, is something that comes with time. Finding and learning to trust your voice can be a fascinating process of exploration and discovery. You are your own source of material. Your experiences, your memories, the people you know or have known, the houses you've lived in, your bad-tempered rabbit that ran away one too many times – these belong to you. They're yours to use in your work, to shape and fashion in new and wonderful ways.

Make notes about You. It can be helpful to take a look at the things that inform you as a writer. It can give you clues to who you are and what your strongest subject matter may be. Using the following list, make some notes about yourself. This is a very revealing exercise, so take some time and see what you can find about the cultural forces that are shaping you.

- Gender
- Place
- Age
- Nationality
- Language
- Religion
- Culture (21st century capitalism)
- Subculture: bogan, westie, goth, surfie, hippie, indie?
- Politics
- Star sign
- Architecture
- Class

- Travel / mobility
- Sexual preference
- Physical attributes
- Disability
- Health
- Food
- Job
- Education
- Dreams
- Family
- Rites of passage
- Birth/death/loss
- Friends

Alfred Kazan says, 'So one writes to make a home for oneself on paper ... to write is to live again, and in this personal myth and resurrection of our experience, to give honour to our lives.'

Write a piece about the place you come from, or about the place you are living now.

Write about:

* Toes

* The green sofa

* Blossoms

* Winter

* Yesterday

* My island

* A good friend

* A bad habit

* Porridge

* Scary sunsets

* Being wonderful

* A new religion

* Moonblossoms

* My relationship to sticky cakes

* Being old/young/mad/sorry/weird

* Two radiant dancers and a ruined piano

The five senses

Everything we are is taken in through our five senses. This is how the world comes to us. It is vital to stay alive to the information we receive through the windows of what we taste, touch, hear, smell and see.

Seeing is important. That's why I like walking. I try not to think as I walk, to inhabit my body instead of my head, filling my lungs with clean air and feeling my feet on the good earth. Seeing things opens me up in ways it's not always easy to explain. I just walk and look. A yard scattered with ugly garden gnomes. A boy with a wonky grin. Who knows what will find a home in a poem one day or manifest in my next chapter.

Other times I find inspiration by visiting an art gallery. Sometimes the magic is that a particular painting or concept stimulates me. Again, it's not always easy to enunciate how the five senses feed your writer's mind, but they do. In the art galleries of Europe, full of masterpieces, the painting I remember best is a one of a turnip. I loved that turnip. Elegant, simple and spare. Will this experience be given to a character in one of my books? Or was it that the simplicity reminded me to aim for elegant simple sentences, not grandiosity or melodrama in my work? These are questions that don't need answers. Looking is important. Use your eyes.

Make room for everything. Maybe it won't be the painting that feeds your creativity. It might be the details of people you observe in the park afterwards: the sad droop of a skirt, the unusual hair of the talkative man.

Interesting postcards and photographs provide good stimulus for writers. Recently at the Balmain Market I bought a packet of old photographs. I don't even know why yet. They seem to be taken in one family, over many years, some in Europe, some in Australia. I see the same faces, over the years. There are many photographs of fathers and sons. One day I'll write something based on those evocative pictures.

Pick a song – one with interesting lyrics. Try Paul Kelly. Try jazz, rap, a sad love song. Don't think, just free-flow write, responding from your belly not your brain. Sometimes writing to music with no lyrics is good, so experiment with music playing softly in the background.

Here is a beautiful piece of writing that involves hearing.

'In the darkness, the town gave forth the sounds of its invisible life: a dog yelping, shouts, a radio badly tuned, an inconsolable child crying, a motor scooter puttering down a potholed lane, the drubbing of an initiation drum.'

Michael Jackson, *The Accidental Anthropologist: A Memoir*

Write a self-portrait using all five senses.

- ↝ Write your morning as a landscape
- ↝ Write your morning as a soundscape

Play around with the following:

- ✍ I smell like (peanut butter and old roses)
- ✍ I sound like (crazy wind through rusty wire)
- ✍ I taste like (mud? melon and ocean?)
- ✍ I hear (elves chanting and windows creaking)
- ✍ My skin feels like (old velvet)

Names

How did you get your name? Most people have a story
behind the name they were given. In my case, I was one
of four daughters. When my first sister was born, my
parents planned to call her Brigid but my grandmother
discouraged it, saying that Brigid, or Biddy as it was often
shortened to in Ireland, was a servant's name. So they
called my oldest sister Robin. Similarly, they bowed to my
grandmother's wishes and named their next two daughters
Judy and Vanya. However, by the time I came along, ten
years later, my parents decided that it was time to use the
name they'd always had a fondness for (and time to ignore
my grandmother), so Brigid is my name. Another story
about names in my family is that we weren't given middle
names. We were just Robin, Judy, Vanya and Brigid, plain
and simple, until the day my oldest sister came home from
school with a piece of work signed Robin Pansy Primrose
Violet Lowry. I understood her desire. I would have loved
to have had a glamorous middle name, such as Gloria
or Angelina.

Write a piece about how or why you were given your
name. If no family story springs to mind, make one up. Or

write about what you would have preferred to be called, if you don't much like the name you have been given.

Choosing good names for the characters in your stories is a creative act in itself. The chosen name needs to suit the character, and you need to watch out for similar names, which will confuse the reader, eg, Carla and Carol, or Mick and Nick.

Use your name as a verb. *Doing a Brigid*, for example, means writing lots of lists about what I *could* do instead of actually doing anything. *Doing a Sam* means leaving an assignment to the very last minute, then staying up all night with a large pot of coffee and writing something magnificent that gets an 'A'. *Doing a Nick* means laughing boisterously and randomly during maths to disconcert the relief teacher. Insert your own name or the name of your friend. What is *Doing an Emily*?

Write a piece about your name, inspired by the following extract from *The House on Mango Street* by Sandra Cisneros. 'In English my name means hope. In Spanish it means too many letters. It means sadness. It means waiting. It is like the number nine. A muddy colour. It is the Mexican records my father plays on Sunday mornings when he is shaving, songs like sobbing.'

Write an alphabet of names using fanciful and whimsical descriptions. Feel free to base it on the following, from *Tomorrow All Will be Beautiful*:

An alphabet of girls with glorious names

A Languid in pale satin, a girl sits writing in a green Chinese notebook. She writes her own name, trying out styles and possibilities: *Anna, Annabelle, Annalisa, Annie*. She doodles a star, a heart, a cloud. She plays with words. Acrobat, she writes, avenue, artichoke, abacus.

B My name is *Bella*, which means beautiful. My mother, Beatrice, says I'm lovely but mothers tell tender lies, to make their children feel better. I don't always feel beautiful.

C Chloe dwells in cyberspace. She lives in her bedroom, texting. She's becoming plasma pale.

D Dogs, dusk, dewdrops, diamonds. I'm *Daisy*. I love dragonflies darting, old clothes tumbling, new ideas sprouting.

All about names

How many writers have written pieces involving names? Do some research. Here are a few leads. Terry Whitebeach has two neat poems on the topic: 'My Name' and 'Names.' Try Pablo Neruda's beautiful love poem, 'Matilda', or 'Names' by Billy Collins, dedicated to those who lost their lives on September 11th and to the survivors.

Renaming the vast world

Rename yourself.

Rename your city, street, house, favourite band.

Create new names for the people in your family, your circle of friends or your class. Is your uncle best suited to being called Hedgehog, or Michael-Lost-the-Plot Smith? I just named a few of my friends: Dandelion Dancer, Inkyfingers, Pencil Person, Moonblossom, Hat Man. Be inspired by Terry Whitebeach. She introduced me to Mark-want-to-be-a-warrior, son of Dad-know-it-all, and Jenny-travel-a-lot, daughter of Annette-Spicy-Hot.

In *Poemcrazy*, Suzanne Goldsmith Woodridge tells of her work teaching creative writing in prisons, psychiatric hospitals and juvenile detention centres all around America. It's one of my favourite writing books. If you're interested in words, poems, life, laughter and language, I suggest you find a copy immediately, because the stories and exercises will nourish and inspire you for many moons. One of my favourite activities in the books is a fabulously freeing exercise whereby you rename things. Give it a try. Walk around your room, renaming. A dirty sock becomes blue sky, a window is renamed peaches, a CD cover is now called a hailstorm. You can even stick labels on things if the spirit moves you. Let yourself be playful with language, for the spirit of play will slide into your work and make miracles.

Write a short story in which the reader has to work hard because you have renamed the objects in it. A sofa becomes a whopsitter. A shoe becomes a fongle.

Quirky, weird and strange

One must have chaos in oneself in order to give birth to a dancing star. Friedrich Nietzsche

In the everyday world we live our everyday lives. Here in this necessary place, hereby to be known as Ordinaryville, we must be rational, reasonable and polite. Here we are obliged to do everyday stuff, like waking up, remembering which day of the week it is, cleaning our teeth and endeavouring to get to school on time. Being sensible is all well and good, but wonderful writing doesn't come from an ordinary mind. It comes from the place Natalie Goldberg calls 'wild mind', a deeper place altogether, a land which smells of chocolate and tastes like winter.

If you're bored with your writing, and your work feels stale and lifeless, you need to find ways to go deeper.

Letting yourself live more freely is important in the world of creativity. Ross Bolleter is a composer, poet and musician. He wears interesting shirts and a trademark black hat which makes him look like a Russian émigré at the turn of the last century. His messy kitchen houses a collection of ruined pianos. His life reflects his love of unusual things, which in turn feeds the music he plays and the poetry he writes.

Famous writers of the past have had some very strange habits. Diane Ackerman wrote about this in an article called 'Courting the Muse'. Apparently Schiller sniffed rotten apples, believing that their musty smell helped him work. And Colette began her day by picking the fleas from her cat.

The world would be a dull place indeed if writers, artists and musicians tried to be more sensible. Imagine Tom Waits without his melancholy, or Madonna without her diverse personas. If you want to be a writer, it is your duty to pay homage to the richly peculiar side of life. Your creativity and imagination will blossom as you begin exploring and experimenting with the wacky, the wondrous, the upside-down and the odd.

Let's hit it for strange!

The following starters are intended to encourage you into more original thinking. Your mantra for today is quirky. What is your most bizarre habit? (Mine is treading on every piece of food I see on the pavement when I'm walking. Corn chips are particularly satisfying. I avoid anything squishier than a sandwich.)

* Who is the oddest person you know?

* What is the weirdest thing you ever saw?

* What is the weirdest thing you ever did?

* Describe the world's most interesting breakfast cereal.

* Write a thousand word story about a world in which one important ingredient is missing. How would life be if there were no mirrors? How about a world with no smiling? Or a land where nobody had any fingers?

* Write a story set in a very ordinary house in which one thing is completely out of the ordinary. A bad-tempered talking goldfish? A chair that has healing powers?

Bend a proverb or a common saying out of shape, and let it lead you into a story.

* *The rolling stones were gathering plenty of moss and so were the tiny pebbles because on Wednesday...*
* *People in glass houses shouldn't throw stones, however throwing cheesecake is really really fun...*

Wordplay. Emulate Frank Muir and Dennis Norden. These clever wordsmiths had a radio program called 'My Word!' They told wildly inventive short stories that ended with a cleverly mangled version of a proverb, such as 'You can't have your kayak and eat it too.' Give it a try.

Flip your thinking. It can also be useful to do things differently. Making small changes in your life can lead you into new and interesting places. How can you be inventive in ways which will make your perceptions new and fresh? Rearrange your bedroom? Learn Spanish? Wear only one colour all weekend?

- ❖ Walk home from school via an unfamiliar route. Imagine making a map for goblins as you go, or how you would describe the journey to a blind person.

- ❖ Write a page using the hand you don't usually use. (Apparently this kicks the more creative, less rational side of your brain into action.)

Try new locations. Writing in an unusual place can also be a way to get you out of a dull patch. Take your journal or your laptop and try somewhere different. I like writing in cafés. Other writers like the beach, or railway stations. What works for you? Maybe you will produce your best work in the bath.

Don't think. Go for a run or a gentle walk. Just stay in your body with the good earth beneath your feet and the wide sky above you. Let the world offer itself to your imagination, as poet Mary Oliver advised. Just be with it all. The fat fluffy cat, the squashed lizard, the smell of fried onions wafting from an open window. Then go back to your desk and write.

About reading

I will never forget learning to read. Back when I was really small, words scurried past my eyes like little black beetles trying to get away from me. But I was too clever for them. I learned to recognise them no matter how fast they ran.
Margaret Mahy

Wear the old coat and buy the new book. Austin Phelps

Life-transforming ideas have always come to me through books.
bell hooks

Outside of a dog, a book is Man's best friend. Inside of a dog it's too dark to read.
Groucho Marx

Always read stuff that will make you look good if you die in the middle of it.
P.J. O'Rourke

I have always imagined that paradise will be a kind of library.
Jorge Luis Borges

If you want to be a writer, you have to be a reader too. No ifs, buts and maybes. You probably don't need to be told this. Do you take books into the toilet with you? Do you carry one, or more, in your backpack? Are there seventeen books scattered on the floor by your bed? Do you haunt bookshops and libraries? Do you check out people's bookshelves to see if they have any good stuff you can borrow? These are the tell-tale signs. Be warned: It's an addiction. It can't be cured and it will probably get worse.

Stephen King says the two main things you have to do if you want to be a successful author is write a lot and read a lot. He calls reading the creative centre of a writer's life, and advises that you take a book wherever you go. He says you need to learn to read in sips as well as long swallows, and he reads anywhere he can, including at the dinner table and in queues. While driving, he listens to books on tape. He doesn't do it because he should; he does it because he loves reading. It feeds him as a person and as a writer, in invisible ways, as well as in obvious ones.

Reading is a life-affirming act. When we read we are joined to other people, some of them long dead. Through reading, the history of the world becomes our own. It is a huge gift to understand someone you don't know, to have them reach out and touch your heart and mind, by the power of what they've written.

Certain books change lives. In World War II, a young American man, Robert Aitken, was captured and interred in a Japanese prisoner of war camp. His only reading material was a tattered copy of R.H. Blythe's *Zen in English Literature*, lent to him by one of the guards. The young man read it innumerable times. Later he had the good fortune to meet Blythe himself in the same camp and got a first hand introduction to haiku and Zen from him. When the war ended, Robert Aitken went to Japan and studied Zen. He later became a Zen Roshi. With his wife, Anne, he founded a Zen centre in Hawaii and, now an old man, he is one of the world's foremost Zen scholars and haiku translators. The book he read changed his life, just as the books he writes will change other lives. Such is the power of reading.

How you read

Apart from the pure joy and delight of reading, there are ways you can read that will be of great use to you as a writer. Francine Prose says, in *Reading Like a Writer*, that part of a reader's job is to find out why certain writers endure. This doesn't mean that every best-selling author is a brilliant stylist, far from it. However, many great writers are great because they use language in the finest way possible. Prose suggests taking particular note of first sentences. Is it a complex introductory one that sets the tone for the entire work to follow? Is it full of bravado and playful assurance, or sombre and tear-stained? Does it startle you with how much sheer storytelling it contains? Prose says she has a special shelf of books whose writers have polished each superb sentence to perfection. When she feels her own writing is getting sluggish or lazy, she takes down a book, say Raymond Carver, and begins to read, letting the magnificence of good writing lift her from the doldrums.

It can be a good thing to ask questions of a text as you read it. Some possible questions might be:

- Did the beginning hook me in immediately?

- Is the plot sustained and well-developed?

- Is the style fluent and controlled?

- Are the characters credible and developed?

- Does the story feel clichéd and familiar? Or original and juicy?

- Is there anything especially noteworthy about the voice, style, punctuation, use of dialogue?

- Do the sentences vary in length?

- Does the author use any device particularly well, eg, sensuous detail? Metaphors and similes?

- Is the ending satisfying and believable?

Reading twice

Reading a poem, story or novel twice can be useful. The first time, just read. Respond to what you read with your heart. Relax and enjoy. On the second reading, you can be more analytical. What devices did the writer use? What worked? What didn't? This type of critical reading can be immensely helpful, but don't let it spoil that first fresh reading for pure pleasure.

Lawrence Durrell says he reads 'not only for pleasure, but as a journeyman, and where I see a good effect I study it, and try to reproduce it.' Durrell isn't recommending plagiarism. To steal or blatantly copy another writer is not only immoral, it's illegal and maybe even fattening. But studying the styles of other writers can teach you a lot. By enjoying, exploring and analysing the work of other writers, you'll extend your own knowledge base. Be bold when you read. Read African novelists, Japanese poets, cyberpunk blogs, picture books, comedy, tragedy, film scripts and comic strips. Let the wonderful world of words and ideas inform you as a reader and as a writer. There's a whole journey of meaning ahead of you if you read with your mind as well as your heart.

As one of my favourite t-shirt sayings laments:
So many books, so little time.

Exercises

Next time you read a book, choose one thing and observe how the writer handles it, eg, sentence structure, adjectives, dialogue. If it's your own copy, you can mark things that interest you with a pencil or a highlighter. If it's a library book, best not.

Today I got four books out of the library. Here are the first four lines. Two of them work better for me, as invitations into the text. What do you think? Which ones do you like, and why?

'As the wind blows through our bedroom window, it sounds like a whistling tea kettle.'

Adriana Trigiani, *Home to Big Stone Gap*

'Our bed was shaking and it woke me up afraid.'

Michael Kimball, *How Much of Us There Was*

'The sun makes its orange way east from Arabia, over the Red Sea, across volcanic hills and desert and over the black hills to the quat- and coffee-shrubbed land of the fertile valley that surrounds our walled city.'

Camilla Gibb, *Sweetness in the Belly*

'Oftentimes on summer evenings, I would sit outside with my mother and look at the constellations.'

Elizabeth Berg, *We Are All Welcome Here*

THREE
JUICY STUFF

stomach
belly
(tummy)
gut?
abdomen

What I like:
Roses, beach, music, sleeping in,
old hippie clothes, chocolate anything,
late nights, reading, clouds

What I don't like:
Raisons in curry, cold coffee,
being told what to wear,
dog-shit on my shoe, adults who
talk about what a mess the
world is in but do nothing about it,
runny eggs

NGS THAT ARE SLOW
ndays
epy snails
bons
nting Roads
mbies
rtoises

' message

Real juicy

It is important to tell the truth. This means the truth as you know it. On one level writing is about telling lies and getting paid for it. You build on the firm ground of experience and from that solid basis you make it up as you go along. However, the essence of truth must be present if your writing is to have validity and resonance.

Tell it like it is. If visiting your grandmother is an experience you dread, and you choose to write about it, then tell it like it is. Your story must have sorrow in it, and a lurking cat that jumps on the bench, leaving a hair in the butter. You need to describe the sad salad of tired lettuce so that the reader experiences the misery of a girl who is eating her lunch very slowly. She's pretending to enjoy it but she's itchy with the guilt of wishing she were somewhere else. If you write about a happy girl visiting her charming grandmother, you are cheating the reader, and yourself.

Part of honest writing is avoiding clichés. A cliché is any word, sentence or idea that you have heard before. A good writer needs to find new ways to describe things that have been described many times before. Can you give the reader the way it feels to love someone who doesn't love you, in a fresh original way? Or the look of a red rose or a rainy night? Sometimes originality will come to you straight away, sometimes you will have to dig long and hard to find it.

Natalie Goldberg suggests asking yourself what it is you really want to say when you can feel that your writing is getting duller and duller. This question can take you from treading water to the bottom of the ocean. Try asking it next time you realise you are writing tired borrowed words, and feel your writing deepen.

Honest writing has great power. It connects you to yourself and to other people. As J.D. Salinger said, 'What really knocks me out is a book that, when you're all done reading it, you wish the author that wrote it was a terrific friend of yours and you could call him up on the phone whenever you felt like it.' Certain songs, poems, books or films make you feel glad to be alive. They feel as though they were created just for you. These texts are honest, fresh and juicy, and they are created when people speak in a voice that is true.

When I taught writing at Curtin University, I knew from the moment Jaya entered the classroom that she was a juicy person. She wore wildly creative clothing and dreads adorned with shells. Jaya's writing was original, fresh and strong. When she was travelling in Japan, her emails were wonderful tales of the ordinary made extraordinary, like the miso soup that was meant to be vegetarian but had a tiny dried fish floating in the bottom. Even a temple in the snow becomes vivid when Jaya describes it.

The following is one of my favourite Jaya pieces.

A Small Prayer

A feral boy wanders into my market stall and asks for a flyer to the next poetry reading. He is dark and beautiful. I wonder what it would be like to rub myself up against his skin. A friend said she saw him snogging a girl with hairy legs at a Ben Harper concert once.

I like feral boys with pumpkin flares, chicken elbows and fish hands flapping. I have a feeling for boys who plant trees and vegetables, who know the names of growing things. I like them with their fingers firmly planted in my earth, bodies like skinny tree trunks, corduroy trousers stained with mud.

I like girls with hairy legs, pieces of land that have been reforested. In them the world is pristine, rising up renewed like it was for the first time.

May all girls with hairy legs be well and happy.
May all boys who snog girls with hairy legs be well and happy.
May all that lives be well and happy.

You can see how original writing takes you somewhere you have never been before. It invites you in and makes you want more!

Exercises

* Write a prayer of your own.

* You wake up one morning to find you've been given an airline ticket to the three places in the world you most want to visit. Thus begins an amazing journey. Record your travels in the form of emails, postcards, a travel journal, an interior monologue, a series of phone calls or any other form that feels good.

Starters

* If I had magical powers…
* Beautiful people, ugly noses
* Kiss chasey in a green Hillman
* Save it for someone who believes you
* Fairy dust and elf powder
* Fear of water
* Handbags I have known
* The land of blue socks
* Mr Hermoley wept
* The best motel
* Beyond flowers and money
* Soup, toast and loneliness
* Daytime television
* Once I loved…
* Dressed in an old satin kimono…

Words

Stories, like people and butterflies and songbirds' eggs and human hearts and dreams, are also fragile things, made up of nothing stronger or more lasting than twenty-six letters and a handful of punctuation marks.
Neil Gaiman

A word is not a crystal, transparent and unchanged, it is the skin of a living thought and may vary greatly in colour and content according to the circumstances and the time in which it is used. Oliver Wendell Holmes, Jr.

It's fun to talk with someone who doesn't use long, difficult words but rather short easy words like 'What about lunch?' A.A. Milne, in *Winnie the Pooh*

Words ought to be a little wild, for they are the assault of thoughts on the unthinking. John Maynard Keynes

As far as I'm concerned, 'whom' is a word that was invented to make everyone sound like a butler.
Calvin Trillin

Words are your building blocks. You might think that this fact is so incredibly simple it isn't worth saying it, but it's vital. Words are the writer's tools of trade and you need to develop a deep respect for them if you wish to write well. Language may be only partial, but it's all you've got to tell a story. Cultivate a love of words, collect them, delight in them. Each and every word must be the very best one for the job you want it to do. Good writing is built on this. All you have to do is find the right word, put it in the right place, over and over again until you die.

Here's an example, from Isabelle Allende's memoir, *My Invented Country*. Allende describes the rambling mansion she was born in, as 'vast and drowsy'. Technically, a house isn't drowsy but the use of the word drowsy in that sentence is unique. It lifts her description into the realms of juicy writing. Allende's memoir, which weaves memories of life and family with observations about Chile, would have been a fairly ordinary account if not for her marvellous use of language. Another example: Allende describes her beloved grandfather as a gentleman who'd drag himself painfully out of his chair to welcome a guest even 'to the end of his days, when he was nothing but a bundle of old bones and leather.' Imagine if she'd written that her grandfather was old but still got up to greet visitors. It's not the same, is it? When used skilfully, language packs a powerful emotional punch.

Parts of speech

Just in case you were communing with the clouds that day in English, here's what I remember from *my* school days about parts of speech.

Nouns stand for things. A noun is a naming word. It can name a person, animal, place, thing, or an abstract idea. If you can touch it, it's a noun: table, shoe, cup, rose, handbag, nose, paper, rock, scissors. Some nouns can't be touched, such as moon, or love. If a noun needs a capital letter, it's called a **proper noun**. People and places are proper nouns: Sam Field, New Mexico, Hudson River.

Pronouns are little words that stand for proper nouns, such as he, she, him, me, her. They can be handy, so tuck several in your pocket today. When choosing nouns, be specific. Say slipper instead of footwear, peacock instead of bird.

Adjectives are words that describe nouns. For example: black, sparkly, ancient, merciless, haggard, sleepy. Consider carefully whether using an adjective will strengthen or weaken your sentence.

Verbs are doing words: kiss, leap, wander, skate, cook, ride. Strong verbs make strong writing.

Adverbs are words that modify verbs. They often end in 'ly'. Adverbs indicate manner, time, place, cause, or degree. They answer questions such as when, how, where, and how much. Examples: slowly, soon, calmly, lately, plenty. Using too many adverbs makes for flabby writing. Please never have a character laugh mischievously, or cry sadly, or I shall have to hit you with a wet fish.

My computer just told me there are eight parts of speech but to be honest, I've totally forgotten what participles, prepositions and conjunctions are. I seem to get by quite nicely. Feel free to Google them up, look in your dictionary, or ask my editor.

Always remember to use strong verbs, careful adjectives and blow adverbs out of the water. I stole this sensible line from my friend, writer Fleur Beale.

Fleur Beale (proper noun) lives (verb) quietly (adverb) in Island Bay (proper noun). Fleur likes dark (adjective) chocolate (noun), travel (noun) and texting (verb) her lovely (adjective) daughters (noun) Penny and Bridget (proper nouns).

Words stand for ideas and feelings. When you're choosing nouns, concrete nouns – such as diamond, hamburger and sky – have the strongest impact. These good solid nouns tend to go with showing. Be wary and more sparing with your use of abstract nouns, such as love, hope, truth. These tend to go with telling. I was told in a writing workshop that you can only use an abstract noun if you've already purchased ten concrete ones. Not a bad ratio, actually.

Jason Rekulak, in *The Writer's Block*, gives a great example of the importance of choosing the right word. Each of the following refers to the same part of your body but you'll create a very different tone or meaning, according to which word you choose – stomach, belly, tummy, gut, abdomen. So, you want to describe the guy who was hanging around outside the railway station on Friday night. Was he evil, dodgy, sleazy, pathetic or malevolent? Each of those words has a subtle nuance, or flavour. Consider exactly what it is that you wish to say, and choose your words accordingly.

Poet Pablo Neruda is a brilliant wordsmith. He writes that words 'glitter like coloured stones, they leap like silver fish, they are foam, thread, metal, dew' and he points out that a whole idea changes if one word shifts, or another settles down 'like a spoiled little thing inside a phrase that was not expecting her.' Neruda reminds us how important it is to work and rework a sentence until every word is in exactly the right place. Take his advice. Treat words like precious objects. Your writing will shine.

The exact word. It can take patience to find the exact word you need. Take your time finding the word you want. If you aren't sure, leave a gap and fill it in later. Slow down and pay attention to words, the raw material from which your work is crafted, and find the one you really want. Be warned, the right word often comes at the oddest moment, like when you're nearly asleep, or waiting in line in the supermarket.

In *Poemcrazy*, Suzanne Goldsmith Woodridge encourages students to make word collections, which she calls wordpools. A wordpool can contain big or small words, foreign words, misspelled words, anything your heart desires. If you collect enough of them, they'll begin to form themselves into poems all by themselves, eg, blue umbrella miracle, harvest green wind. (I chose *Guitar Highway Rose* as a title because it felt like a small poem that embodied the spirit of my novel, in just three words.)

One of the most frequently asked questions of a search engine is 'how many words in the English language?' *The Oxford English Dictionary* lists about 400,000, although some are multiple versions of the same word. Add to that all the words that aren't in the dictionary: slang, foreign terms in common use, new words that are just coming into being. Some experts say there are 500,000 words in English, but they can never be catalogued in a definitive way because language is always in flux. What an amazing range of words to choose from. If you dip and dive in a dictionary you will find some fascinating words, such as *accismus*, pronounced *ak-SIZ-muhs*. It's a noun, and it means feigning disinterest in something while actually desiring it.

The Dictionary. Dictionaries can help in research, especially if you're writing something historical. Some of the words used in earlier times are fascinating; others are hilarious. The following come from a dictionary of vulgar language, circa 1811.

Beau-nasty: *a slovenly fop; grandly dressed, but dirty.*
Cap acquaintance: *persons slightly acquainted, someone you would salute with your hat on meeting.*
Catchfart: *a footboy; who follows closely behind his master or mistress.*
Dew Beaters: *feet.*

Ditto: *a suit of ditto; meaning a coat, waistcoat and breeches, all of one colour.*

Gluepot: *a parson, who joins men and women in matrimony.*

Inexpressibles: *breeches.*

I'm fascinated by words that we don't have in English but which exist in other languages. The most common example of this is the many words Eskimos have for describing various types of snow. Snow is vitally important in Eskimo culture so there are words for dangerous snow, delicate snow, melting snow and other snow formations.

If you're interested in words from other languages that we don't have in English, check out *They Have a Word for it: A Lighthearted Lexicon of Untranslatable Words and Phrases.* You'll learn that the Italians have a word for a bore who corners people with sad pointless tales. Germans have *schadenfreude*, which is the slight glow of pleasure you feel when something bad happens to someone you don't like. There's a Russian word, *razlyubit*, which describes the feeling for someone you've once loved but now do not. If you hurt yourself in Norway, someone might yell *uffda!* which is a word of sympathy for someone in pain. Another German word that could come in handy is *drachenfutter* (literally dragonfodder), which means a peace offering from a guilty husband to his wife. Japanese have words for concepts that we lack, such as *wabi*, the beauty of simplicity, and *shibui*, meaning restrained elegance. *Eraritjaritjaka* comes from an Aboriginal language and means a desperate looking for something that is lost. Another of my faves is

Yiddish: *farpotshket*. It means something that is all fouled up, especially as the result of an attempt to fix it.

Exercises

Open a dictionary or a poetry book and start a story based on the first word you see.

Summer afternoon, summer afternoon. Henry James said these were the most beautiful words in the English language. What are yours?

Take a poem, blank out some of the nouns and adjectives. Leave it for a week or two, then rebuild it, putting new words in the blank spaces.

Browse in a dictionary. Browse in a dictionary of another language. Spanish and Italian are particularly good. Immerse yourself in the world of words, in the possibilities of language.

Invent some phobias and give them suitable names. The English language has some amazing words for phobias, or the morbid fear or aversion to something. Here are a few examples:

Papyrophobia: fear of paper
Leukophobia: fear of the colour white
Isolophobia: fear of solitude
Logophobia: fear of words
Noctiphobia: fear of the night
Cremnophobia: fear of precipices

Invent new meanings for common words.
Here are some examples from *The Washington Post*'s
annual neologism competition, where readers invent new
meanings for everyday words.

Lymph (verb): to walk with a lisp

Coffee (noun): the person upon whom one coughs

Flatulence (noun): emergency vehicle that picks you up
after you're run over by a steamroller

Pokemon (noun): a Rastafarian proctologist

Invent some new religions of your own.
Have you heard of frisbeetarianism (noun)? It's the belief
that, when you die, your soul flies up onto the roof and
gets stuck there.

Invent some new words and give them
meanings. For example:

A shallot: someone who continually forgets their sports
uniform

Barniveropity: giving money to terrible buskers to get
them to stop playing

Topiferous: someone who looks fabulous in hats

Mix and match. There are languages that go with
disciplines, such as medicine, architecture, politics.
Particular endeavours, like swimming, cooking, skating,
sewing, also have their own languages. Make lists of words
that go with a field of study, or a pursuit, then write a piece

mixing the languages. Try the language of real estate mixed with the language of soccer, for example.

More wondrous quotes about words

It is with words as with sunbeams, the more they are condensed, the deeper they burn.   Robert Southey

A word is not the same with one writer as with another. One tears it from his guts. The other pulls it out of his overcoat pocket.   Charles Peguy, poet and essayist

A man who uses a great many words to express his meaning is like a bad marksman who, instead of aiming a single stone at an object, takes up a handful and throws at it in hopes he may hit.

        Samuel Johnson, lexicographer

The difference between the right word and the nearly right word is the same as that between the lightning and the lightning bug.   Mark Twain

Metaphors and similes

Young man, take a haircut. You look like a chrysanthemum.   P.G. Wodehouse

A **simile** is a word that compares something to something else. It's indicated by the use of the word *like*. For example, her smile was like a watermelon.

A **metaphor** links something to something else imaginatively, eg, the big bowl of the sky.

Metaphors and similes are everywhere. They can be wonderful, they can be horridly clichéd, they can be mysterious or clear, maddening or insightful. Stale metaphors and similes will drag your work down, but good ones will give it real zing.

Here are two examples from *Tanglewreck* by Jeanette Winterson. The first is a simile. The woman 'whipped out her compact to powder her nose. It was like dust settling on a rock.' The next is a metaphor. 'Chocolate cake thick as a mattress.'

Poet and author, Jessica Le Bas, refines and expands her

way with words by underlining metaphors and similes as she reads. She found 114 similes and metaphors in *Black Swan Green* by David Mitchell, which, by the way, is a terrific coming-of-age-story about an adolescent boy with a stutter. *Black Swan Green* is written in the first person and is semi-autobiographical. I highly recommend it. Here's an example I liked: 'The bones in her neck were standing out like scaffolding.'

Terence Hodgson collects similes and metaphors. His book, *Eyes Like Butterflies*, groups them according to subject, eg, Hair, Rain, Eyes, Face, Smiles, Houses. Here is a selection. Which ones work for you?

His hair was that special mad yellow, like an omelette –
    Martin Amis, *Money*
Hair careful as a hat – Peter Vansittart, *Quintet*
A bewitching of rain – Janet Frame, *The Edge of the Alphabet*
A soft antique rain – Ann Kavan, *Sleep Has its House*
Sabres of black rain – John Banville, *Birchwood*
Dawn of broken eggs and oyster shells – Anthony Burgess,
    Napoleon Symphony
Eyes like trespassers – Peter Vansittart, *Landlord*
Face like a good-natured bun – Anne Mulcock, *Landscape
    With Figures*
Her long cupboard of a face – Patrick White, *The Vivesector*

Exercises
Read like Jessica Le Bas. Take notice of metaphors and similes when you read.

How many metaphors can you find for memory? Here are a few of mine: The flabby corridors of memory. The dusty roads of memory. Memory's mocking laughter.

Create similes or metaphors for a smile.

Here are a few to get you started, from *Eyes Like Butterflies*.

The long thin knife of memory – Matt Cohen, *The Bookseller*

A smile like a torch with a weak battery – Hugo Charteris,
  The Indian Summer of Gabriel Murray

Housebroken smile – Penelope Shuttle, *Rainsplitter in the
  Zodiac Garden*

Her smile was so wide she might have been related to the
  sun – Michael Field, *The Short Cut Life of Bacchus Pocock*

Take similes and turn them into metaphors:

Her hair was like a waterfall. Her waterfall hair.
The day was smooth as silk. Silk smooth day.

Make a list of twenty strong nouns: radio, moon, life, highway, chaos, basketball, sneaker, knife, star. Then make a list of adjectives: tired, joyous, blue, lost, magical, faded. Now, combine a word from each list to create imaginative metaphors and similes.

✳ The fat basketball moon.
✳ The wet highway of his smile.
✳ Her life was blue chaos.

Lists

Lists are a popular device in literature. You can use one to describe a character, a morning, a life, a universe. Lists can be poetic, funny, sensible, weird. They're a wonderful way to condense language.

Lists have always been a favourite device of mine. I didn't plan to be the queen of lists, but I love them, and I used them extensively in my book *Guitar Highway Rose*. Rosie, one of the main characters, was partly created by listing her likes and dislikes.

What I like: roses, beach, music, sleeping in, old hippie clothes, chocolate anything, late nights, reading, clouds

What I don't like: raisins in curry, cold coffee, being told what to wear, dog-shit on my shoe, adults who talk about what a mess the world is in but do nothing about it, runny eggs

Asher was the other main character in *Guitar Highway Rose*. I used the following list to provide the reader with information about him. It may look as if it was a random selection but the items in the list were very carefully chosen. Some tell about the sort of boy Asher is, but the photograph, the half-eaten pear and the empty incense box help set up the reader's mood before the final list item, which is an important foreshadow of the developing plot.

Asher's Bedroom

Futon on the floor with black sheets and white pillows and a black doona. Row of books beside bed – arranged on board balanced on two bricks – including The Hitchhiker's Guide to the Galaxy, two Richard Brautigan books inherited from Nigel, and well thumbed copy of No One Gets Out of Here Alive, the Jim Morrison biography. One old guitar. Two songbooks. Three picks. Six white candles stuck in an assortment of bottles. Ashtray in shape of crocodile. Photo of Asher, Sam, Viv and Jesse, arms around each other, laughing. Batik backpack containing school books. Bamboo rack meant for holding clothes. Clothes on floor. Cassette player and twenty-seven tapes, four still with boxes. Poster of The Doors. Pulp Fiction poster. Sheep skull. Crystal pyramid. Empty sandalwood incense packet. Half-eaten pear. And on the bed, one lonesome boy.

In Follow the Blue I ended the book with twelve character sketches in the form of interior monologues. This was a way of tying up plot ends and giving the reader a satisfying sense of where each character was at. Jaz was one of my favourite people in *Follow the Blue* and I wrote her epilogue in the form of an extended list of things she wants. It was an efficient way to show her exuberant personality, and to articulate her dreams.

Jaz

What I want. I want to get to know Sam better, because he's so cool and he bothers to think for himself. I want to live somewhere brilliant like London or Prague. I want to mix with poets and artists and musicians and circus people. I want to get into the music scene. I want to do things that challenge me. I want to learn to fly, be a DJ, do a kickflip, be an acrobat. I don't want to ever just stay the same. I want my parents to grow up and stop acting dumb, like going for the fast easy dollar, and drinking too much. They've almost forgotten how to be kind. I want them to be happy, but even if they can't I'm not going to let it cripple me. I am a white frangipani blossom that smells like heaven. I am the one and only Jaz.

With Lots of Love from Georgia concludes with a list. My intention with this list was to leave the reader feeling uplifted, amused and satisfied.

Things to do while watching a sunset

sing a Ben Harper song
clean nails with a twig
name the clouds
drink something fizzy and burp a lot
laugh out loud because in 300 years your zits
    will not matter
compose a small poem
play marbles
write your name in air with your finger
pray for world peace
practise winking
make a daisy chain
eat a peach

Exercises

❖ Write your own list of Things To Do While Watching a Sunset

❖ Write a character sketch in the form of a list, a la Jaz

❖ Write a list of things in a bedroom that says a lot about the owner of the room

❖ Write a character sketch that involves a list of what the person likes and does not like

Make lists of:

- Great names for bands

- Things the opposite sex shouldn't be allowed to own

- Bad things to serve at a dinner party

- What the perfect motel room would contain

- Things grandparents should never say

Write a short history of the world in the form of a list.

Describe yourself using a list.

Create a prose poetry piece answering the question: What should I bring? To a picnic, a birthday party, a funeral?

Here's a piece I wrote when I was bored in a writing class:

> Bring along a birthday wish. Bring two pens, in case one runs out. Bring along a library card, two dollars sixty-four, a note book, a giraffe. Bring along anything you can't live without. Bring an umbrella, a suitcase, three chocolate frogs. Bring champagne. A post card. A spare pair of underwear. Bring a half-forgotten secret. An abandoned railway station. A ruby. A night sky. A blade of sweet grass.

Write a poem. In a lovely poem called 'Mothers With A Baby' Guadalupe Morfin itemises things that a mother with a baby needs: a cup of hot soup, a blackboard that will hold a rainbow, a swing, a kite, a unicorn. Use her device to write a poem listing the things you think a mother, or a father, with a baby might need.

The poem 'Angels' by Maurya Simpson is entirely built on lists (except for the last two lines). The author lists types of angels, including those 'who dress in black velvet' and those who 'wince and fidget like bats'. Write a poem about angels, based on her idea. You may also wish to end with two strong lines that are different, as Simpson did, to give your poem oomph, and stop it being 'just a list'.

'Subtotals' by Gregory Burnham, is a short story constructed entirely of a list. The author cleverly constructs a sketch of a man and his entire life by listing the number of times certain things occurred. 'Number of times didn't believe parents 23,978. Number of times choked on bones, chicken: 4; fish: 6; other: 3.'

Write the story of your own life, or someone else's, using the idea of numbers and a list.

Another of my favourite pieces of writing based on a list is by Susan Wicks in *Driving My Father*, which is a candid account of the author's relationship with her elderly father after her mother's death. It's a great book because it's such an honest account of things, not a sugary version. The relationship varies in time and atmosphere, and is cleverly detailed, mixing happy and unhappy memories. The reader is fully engaged because the story is never predictable.

Wicks' skill as a poet is apparent in the following excerpt: 'At every moment somewhere, someone is dying. Someone is reaching down into damp earth. Someone is playing chess. Someone is dancing to unsuitable music.'

Juicy Writing Tip. Wicks follows her lovely poetic list of things people might be doing with a strong statement: 'When people asked me which one of my parents I preferred, I always said my father.' By inserting this powerful statement after her poetic list, she takes the reader by surprise and makes them think. Lifting a text in this way is a good device to incorporate in your own work.

Write a page that begins with the line 'At every moment someone somewhere is…'

Grace Goodfellow is a genius with lists. She has kindly let me show you one of hers, from a novella she's working on:

Things that are slow
Mondays
Sleepy snails
Ribbons
Country roads
Kombis
Tortoises
An ancient computer trying to open up a Word
   document
An old man writing a text message

A bike with a flat tyre
Someone with a hangover
Smiles (in certain situations)
Your mum, when she's trying to decide whether
    to order a Greek or Caesar salad
Clouds on a windless night
Tibetan monks
Sleeping breaths
Breakfast on Saturday morning
Boredom
A picnic on the banks of a quiet river
Intimate kisses
Scrabble
Stifled tears
The arrival of a letter from Poland
Meditation
The world turning
Traffic jams
Stars moving
Unrequited love

Make a list of anything you want to.

Things which are slow, fast, ugly, wonderful, silver. Things
that would improve the world. Things dogs know but people
don't. The sky's the limit when it comes to list making, so get
listing!

Poetry

A poem is a paper boat made of your own words.
Guadalupe Morfin

Prose: words in their best order; poetry: the best words in the best order.
Samuel Coleridge

Poetry is thoughts that breathe, and words that burn.
Thomas Gray

Poetry is a hard thing to define. It is words made special, words put together in interesting ways to make gatherings of words that make us laugh, cry, think, wonder, pause for a while. Poetry is a potent form of language, one in which words are asked to do more than ordinary words.

Carl Sandburg said that 'poetry is a synthesis of hyacinths and biscuits.' A hyacinth is a very elegant blossom, waxy and classical, tall and still, with tiny bell-like flowers. Biscuits are homely, small, brown, crunchy, crumbly. By juxtaposing hyacinths and biscuits, two words that don't usually go together, Sandburg creates an image that is itself a little poem, a place where the listener pauses and the words make an impact. That's the magic of poetry. It creates a space where words form ideas that stop and make us go 'OH.'

A wonderful thing about poetry is that it can be on any subject at all. There are poems about war, Christmas, parents, pets, zits, parties, broken hearts, kites, bicycles, vases, dogs, Autumn, God, gardening. You name it and there's probably been a poem written about it. Poetry is a very big topic. There are thousands and millions of books of poetry in this world today, and thousands and millions of books about poetry. I could write from now until forever about poetry and still have only just begun. Maybe it is good to remember that as Dylan Thomas said, there is no such thing as poetry, only poems.

Poetry or song?

Not everyone likes poetry, but most people like songs, which I consider to be poems put to music. If you like writing song lyrics, you may find reading poetry helpful. Don't limit yourself to the sort of poetry you read. Poems comes in a huge variety of shapes and sizes, ranging from a two-line rhyming couplet to an epic that spans thousands of pages. It can be a light-weight amusing limerick or a nature-inspired haiku that jolts the reader into a new way of seeing. If you want to write poetry, immerse yourself in poems. Try traditional poetry, contemporary poetry, poems by writers of all nationalities. By reading and absorbing, your ability as a poet will improve. It can be fun to try out different forms, like a sestina, or a sonnet, or an epithalamion, which is a poem or song in honour of a bride and bridegroom. I wrote one for my friends, Mari and Allen, when they got married, and it has since been adapted to read at other weddings.

The Wedding Poem

Off you go, you two, off you go.
Away with you, into the dusky summer evening,
flying a light plane into the winds of possibility
    and chance,
into a blue sky abundant
with dreams and credit cards, daughters and dogs,
discussions about microwaves and fairy lights.

Everything in the universe
has led to just this moment.

Off you go, call the friends
as they hold tiny handkerchiefs to their eyes.
They are thinking wistful thoughts of marriages
    gone by.
They are contemplating tricky corners of
    marriages present.
They are wondering softly about marriages yet
    to come.

Off you go, call the friends, away with you, darlings.
Yes indeed, say the families, farewell and god bless,
the family who are here today, those who
    cannot be with us
and the ghosts of the ancestors
backwards into shimmering time.
Yes, yes, we who are gathered here today are
    whispering.
Yes, and utterly yes.

With this we bless you.
Right now we bless you,
we bless you, we bless you,
we utterly bless you.

Write a poem which commemorates a birth, a death, a wedding or another important occasion.

Don't waste a word

You can't afford to waste a single word in a poem. As poet George Crane put it, 'a poem with a word wrong is like a baby without a head. It cannot live.' Or as West Australian poet and editor Wendy Jenkins says, you have to find 'the shortest way home.'

The following poem, a character sketch by Alison Georgeson, is a tiny gem. It is, and it obeys all the rules of juicy writing. Not a word is wasted, the five senses are involved. Reading it, I can almost hear the ivory tiles clicking. Notice the tone of the poem – sadness and love, mixed with the smell of burnt toast.

Mah-Jongg

Not to say that my grandmother
was the best Mah-jongg player in
the world by any means; she wasn't
Chinese. Breaking walls with dragons
and winds, scattering dice over dots
and bamboo, playing flowers against

seasons, and then winning after
plucking the moon from the bottom
of the sea, her wiry face above
the ivory tiles - like little bibles
holding forth in her lavender kitchen
and never once amid the scents of
Ceylon tea and burnt toast did she
murmur regrets, chagrin, or sorrow.

Write a poem that is a tribute to someone you know.

Try Haiku

Haiku is a deceptively simple form of poetry. Don't be fooled. To write a good haiku is an art. In this ancient traditional form, brevity is a key feature. Language and meaning are condensed to their very essence. Haiku consists of one to three lines totalling 17 syllables or less. A 5-7-5 syllable structure is common, although these days the form is more playful and can be experimented with. A haiku should be able to be read aloud in one breath. Haiku must be subtle, and describe rather than prescribe.

Here's one of the shortest haiku I know, written in the 13th century by Basho, a Japanese poet.

Frog on edge of water.
Plop!

I can see a quiet pond, with deep murky water, maybe a lotus blossom floating in it. There's a mossy log and a small slimy green frog, sitting, poised, and then PLOP! in it goes. A few words, written hundreds of years ago, that still resonate today because they're put together so cleverly and leave us with a sound, a picture, an image, the water still rippling on the pond.

Exercises

Here are three haiku by New Zealand poet Nick Williamson.

9am
the spontaneity workshop
begins

late night talk
on the verandah
... the shhh of the sea

splitting pine
I smell
the whole forest

Write three haiku in response to Nick's. The first based on a time of day, the second having reference to the sea, and the third being in some way related to the sense of smell.

The following haiku is by Perth haiku scholar, John Turner.

home from Asia
I kiss
the water tap

Again, short, sharp and delicious. Poets often inspire each

other. When I returned from the USA, where most bread is soft, squishy and white, I responded with:

> home from America
> I kiss
> the Vogel's bread

Write a haiku that involves kissing, or appreciating something.

One of my favourite haiku by Basho is this one:

> the first cold shower;
> even the monkey seems to want
> a little coat of straw.

Write a haiku that contains a living creature, and has a reference to a season or to weather.

Call in the muse

You can't always write a poem to order. Charles Sandburg said that 'ordering a man to write a poem is like commanding a pregnant woman to give birth to a red-headed child.' Poetry tends to arrive when it feels like it. You can encourage it though. Call in the poetry muse by always having your notebook handy, by reading poetry, and by making spaces in your life – such as walking on a beach, in a forest, or through a city, with all your senses alive.

> *It's seeing more than what's there.*
>
> Toni Morrison, *On Poetry*

Food

Tomatoes and oregano make it Italian; wine and tarragon make it French. Sour cream makes it Russian; lemon and cinnamon make it Greek. Soy sauce makes it Chinese; garlic makes it good.   Alice May Brock

As actress Lisa Harrow once said, 'Anyone who doesn't like food, I don't like them.' Hunger is one of the most primal drives, and human beings use food not only to stay alive but to comfort, punish, beguile and show love. Eating can be about family, hunger, nourishment, control, celebration. Cultures are defined in part by the foods that people eat; love affairs have begun with ice-cream or a lavish meal. Funerals are marked with cakes iced with weepy grief, and casseroles presented at a time when words can offer nothing. Our world is rich with stories about food: plums that taste of childhood, Grandad's stew containing a whole lemon, which he learned to cook in Cyprus during the war.

Write about

🚲 A meal that went horribly wrong

⒛ A fabulous feast

⒛ The way my mother cooks an omelette –
The way (fill in the blank) cooks (fill in the blank)

Food is not just food. Here is a poem of mine that starts
with the taste of a red ripe plum, but has themes of loss
and memory.

Plum

I am eating a plum,
this luscious Santa Rosa, fat ruby orb.
Biting, taste long-lost summers,
am a child again
at the fruit stall
by the dusty road to the sea.
Happy girl with strange dreams,
sticky brown hands on a red-stained paper bag.
My parents were alive and summer was forever.
Mouthful of hot sweet memories,
tasting blood sap and remembering.
Here and now
weary years later
I am standing in a kitchen
twelve thousand miles away,
fruit in a bowl, clouds in the sky,
saying yes to a plum.

Write a poem based on a piece of fruit.

Or a bowl of cereal. Or a sausage. Or any other item of
food that takes your fancy.

There can be something wonderfully playful about food. I've just read a list of children's books which have food as a theme. I particularly like the sound of one called *Cloudy With a Chance of Meatballs,* which is set in a town called Chewandswallow where all the food came from the sky. Some days it rains milk, juice or soup; sometimes it snows mashed potatoes. Then comes a terrible storm of giant meatballs with tomato tornadoes! There are many terrific books for younger readers based on food. *Granny Torelli Makes Soup* by Sharon Creech is a delightful story in which Rosie's grandmother teaches her about love, life and lasagne. In Odo Hirsch's *Bartlett and the Ice Voyage* two adventurers set out in search of the rare and delicate melidrop, because the queen is bored with other food. A friend shared this great line with me, 'Queen Felafel and King Babaganoush' and I immediately wished I had written it, so I could turn it into a picture book.

Take the theme of food and pick up your pen, and maybe your paintbox, too.

Let one of these food quotes inspire you to write...

I like reality. It tastes of bread.   Jean Anouilh

Looking for love, she reads cookbooks.   Erica Jong

One cannot live well, love well or sleep well unless one has dined well.   Virginia Woolf

Tell me what you eat, and I will tell you what you are.
                    Anthelme Brillat-Savarin

The most remarkable thing about my mother is that for thirty years she served the family nothing but leftovers. The original meal has never been found.

Calvin Trillin

I went into a McDonald's yesterday and said, 'I'd like some fries.' The girl at the counter said, 'Would you like some fries with that?'

Jay Leno

I like rice. Rice is great if you're hungry and want 2000 of something.

Mitch Hedberg, *Mitch All Together*

Nothing is greater than breakfast. Nothing is more profound than lunch.

Ross Bolleter

A good cook is like a sorceress who dispenses happiness.

Elsa Schiaparelli

It's the Year 2373. Food as we know it has long vanished. **Write a short story** based on this idea.

Create a character based on the contents of their fridge. Or their shopping list.

John Marsden's superb book *Everything I Know About Writing* has a great writing starter based on food. He suggests describing a meal at your house, as narrated by a sports commentator.

It's your last night on death row. What is your last meal?

When I was studying writing at Curtin University, we had a master class with visiting writer-in-residence Tom Shapcott. He was a friendly bear of a man, who produced a banana from his briefcase for each class member, much to our surprise. He then led us solemnly through a series of exercises based on the banana. Describe the banana using all five senses. Describe the banana without using adjectives. Now turn some of your statements into questions. By the end of the class each of the twenty students had written a short story, based on that exercise. If you want to read mine, it's in *Tomorrow All Will Be Beautiful* and it's called 'Tenth Floor'.

Try this exercise yourself and see where it leads you. Any fruit will do.

Novelist and scriptwriter Nora Ephron says that her mother's belief about cooking was that if you worked hard and prospered, someone else would do it for you.

Write a short story which features the life and times of someone who cooks for a living. A caterer on a movie set? A late night worker in a greasy spoon café? A yummy mummy trying to start a business making pickles and chutneys?

Clothing

Clothing provides a wonderful wardrobe for a writer. Our attire simultaneously reveals and conceals many things. What we wear tells us much about ourselves, and literature is abundant with themes of dress and undress. Clothing is a great way to create character. By giving a few details of what a character is wearing, we swiftly gain insight into the sort of person they are. An aunt in her saggy bathing suit, an elderly man whose polyester trousers are too short, a kid at the mall who has all the latest brands but looks very silly.

Clothing can also create mood. Here's an excerpt from *The Lover*, by Marguerite Duras. In just a few words, using the first person, we can not only visualise the character, but get a sense of mood. 'I'm wearing a dress of red silk, but it's threadbare, almost transparent. It used to belong to my mother.' The details of threadbareness and the fact that the dress is a hand-me-down from her mother are details which help create a sense of poignancy. The reader wonders what the relationship is between the girl in the red silk dress and her mother. Later Duras shifts to the third person, as if looking at a photograph of herself. 'It's not the shoes, though, that make the girl look so strangely, so weirdly dressed. No, it's the fact that she's wearing a man's flat-brimmed hat, a brownish pink fedora with a broad black ribbon.' This shift in perspective, and the odd clothes the girl is wearing, bring the character into even clearer visual perspective and continue to build a mood. A very different picture and mood would be created if the girl had neatly brushed hair, a pleated skirt and a pink cardigan.

Clothing can be used to express the character's response to their world. In the following piece, writer Jaya Penelope gives a description of her dancing pants. We not only learn things about the trousers, we learn about the author and her attitude to life.

Dancing Pants. Once I had a pair of dancing pants. They were the colour of green pumpkins, my fringed techno trousers. My pants would dance me around the dance floor. My pants would dance with other people's pants. My pants made rude suggestions. My pants were frisky and risky and everything I was not.

Through the use of a piece of clothing, the reader understands that the wonderful pants are dancing some risky friskiness into being.

Clothing is often used in literature to represent change. I remember throwing my battered panama hat into the hedge, the day I left Epsom Girls' Grammar in December 1969. I was a lumpy grumpy girl of sixteen, with no idea where I was headed in life. But it felt glorious, biffing the hat into that hedge. It wasn't just a hat I was ditching, it was years of rules and regulations, of sitting still and being quiet, of studying dull things. That moment was a celebration of my first day of freedom as I stepped, hatless, into the mystery of my grown-up life.

Hats often appear in my writing, as a representation of bigger things. In 'Alphabetical Destiny', a short story in my collection *Tomorrow All Will Be Beautiful*, a girl describes herself: 'Me with my ragged journal, my daggy flannel nightgowns, my loneliness, my collection of wonderful hats that I was too shy to wear.' The girl in the story has low self esteem. But she idolises her best friend, and again, the relationship is indicated by the way she feels about the other girl's clothes. 'You've got the just-right fluffy cardigan, the ivory bracelets, the bird brooch you scored for three bucks at the markets that turned out to be gold.'

In the following poem of mine, once more the hat is used as a symbolic object, in this case it is an extended metaphor indicating a time of transition.

My Hat

my hat
my new straw hat
cost thirty bucks
wide-brimmed
and circled with black ribbon
beautifully round

a circle a planet an O
it rests on the hook
with the scarf of roses
waiting for summer
for wearing to the river
me and my hat
my wide-brimmed perfect hat
this prop
this item of chance
this flying saucer for the head
In this hat
I become
la contessa
a movie star
my mother before she grew old
I'm poised
on the edge of an afternoon
poised on the edge
of becoming
somebody else.

Clothing can also be used by writers as an indicator of
time and place. Picture a seventeen-year-old boy on his
first day as an insurance clerk in Wellington. It's 1949.
He's wearing a carefully knotted blue tie, very shiny black
shoes and a grey suit that's slightly too small. By including
specific details of what people are wearing, the reader
can see the characters, feel the textures of the fabrics, let
their imaginations create the mood. A girl in India walks

through a market in Mumbai, clad in a bright sari, gilded bracelets on her wrist and a tiny red bindi on her forehead. Can you smell the dusty spices?

Exercises

❧ Create some metaphors and similes based on clothing. For example: her rat's-paradise handbag, her sad-rag skirt; his smelly shoes like gaping caves, my aunt's hat – joyous as a wedding.

❧ Write a piece that describes *A Day in the Life of a Shoe.* Or a scarf, or any other item of clothing.

❧ Take an item of clothing of your own, or one belonging to someone you know. Hold it in your mind's eye, then describe it, using all your senses. What does it feel like, smell like, remind you of? Now let your imagination lead you into a piece of writing. Follow it wherever it decides to go.

❧ If the subject of clothing interests you, I recommend the anthology *Out of Fashion,* edited by Carol Ann Duffy.

FOUR
WRITING ESSENTIALS

WHY?
WHO?
WHEN?
WHERE?
HOW?

CHARACTER

PLOT

Character

Everybody is a universe.   Ang Lee

The two main ingredients to any story are character and plot. These two elements are intimately connected. Each element must be well-developed, and the relationship between the two must be harmonious. The reader must believe in the characters and care what happens to them.

Just as people are ever-evolving, the character in fiction is a work-in-progress. The character's reactions to events are what give the plot its drive. The character must respond as the story unfolds. If the character remains unchanged, there will be no meaningful story.

There are many ways to evoke character. A lengthy detailed description is the most obvious way. In early novels, by authors such as Charles Dickens, a whole page was used to introduce each important character. Although this worked splendidly in those sprawling epic pages, it's less effective in modern fiction. These days a minimal approach is likely to be more successful. Sometimes a small incident or sensuous detail can introduce a character wonderfully well. Let thoughts, tiny details, small actions and significant dialogue speak. Here's a great example by

Gerald Durrell from his book *My Family and Other Animals*. 'Aunt Hermione, an evil old camel smelling of mothballs and fond of singing hymns in the lavatory.' By providing just a few original details, one sentence can say so much.

Originality is important when creating a character. A reader won't care about cardboard cut-outs they've met a hundred times before. Easily recognisable stereotypes such as a plump, smiling, kind grandmother who cooks lovely cakes, or a daffy fourteen-year-old called Kylie who says 'like' in every sentence should be avoided. On the other hand, a character must be coherent. If you strive too hard to make a character quirky and strange, it will be unconvincing. Putting a marijuana plantation in Granny's back yard, or giving Kylie the ability to speak seven languages, including Russian, will just make them implausible, rather than interesting. The aim is to create multi-dimensional characters, unique and believable.

If you want to create compelling characters, don't make them too nice. People are interested in the shadow. For instance, if I tell you my mother was the nicest woman in Auckland, you probably won't be very interested. If, however, I say that my mother was the meanest old bitch in the whole world, I bet you immediately want to know more. Make sure that you give the people who inhabit your work enough grit to make them interesting. (My mother was lovely, by the way.)

Ask questions. In order to be able to write characters, you have to be vitally interested in people. You need to observe people carefully and ask questions. Why did your parents leave Estonia? How do you make cheese? Did you always want to be an actor? If you ask questions, the world will offer you some very juicy stories.

Know your characters. Some writers make copious notes on character before they begin. J.K. Rowling creates detailed histories and complex back stories, not just for Harry Potter, Ron and Hermione but for Parvarti and her more minor characters. Her characters are utterly convincing, millions of fans waited anxiously to hear of their fate in the final book. Rowling is also brilliant at plot, and did a very clever thing by combining magic and boarding school. (She's one of the world's richest women, and yes, I'd like to be her.)

Before Australian author Glynn Parry begins a new young adult book, he cuts interesting faces out of magazines such as *Rolling Stone*. He pins them up in his study, to get a feel for them. Parry then makes index cards about each one, working methodically to create well-rounded, interesting, coherent people.

You need to know your characters well. What do they eat for breakfast? What bores them? What's their most loved item of clothing? What's their favourite song? If you aren't prepared to get to know your people well, to fully believe in them, the chances are the reader won't fully believe in them either. You should be able to make the things they do fit with who they are, because character is built not only by description, but by action and interaction. The key to a character is what they're feeling, and based on their feelings, how they then act. Good stories are about people behaving in ways that the reader will find plausible.

The things people say. Dialogue is a valuable way of showing character. What people say is a guide to who they are, even if they are an unreliable narrator. Showing someone's thought processes by way of an interior monologue can also work well. I used this method when I created Asher, in *Guitar Highway Rose*. I left out all punctuation, flowing with the stream of consciousness that went on inside Asher's head. Many readers have said they could identify with him.

When you create characters they're often based on you, or inspired by people you know. Because of this, it can be hard to give them problems and conflicts. But conflict and thwarted desires are at the heart of story making, so don't protect your beloved creations from harm too carefully, or you may end up with a rather tame story.

Here are two characters created by Grace Goodfellow. She's used the technique of showing what a person is about by telling the reader what they stay away from, and what they think.

'Ollie stays away from angry people, band-aids and cinnamon donuts.'

'Zeph:
I think
That girls are confusing.
Nutella ice-cream is delicious.
Internet has killed, and is killing, the everything star.
I should learn when to stop.
Mosquitoes are more dangerous than you could ever imagine.
Fiddles are brilliant.
And that "they" should reveal their true identities.'

Exercises

Describe someone in two words. (I did this in *With Lots of Love from Georgia*. It was a good way to give the reader more information about the characters, including Georgia.)

In Two Words

Mrs Jakovich
Efficient. Speedy.
Eva
Sulky. Fragrant.
Bob
Dodgy. Gormless.

Hunter
Interesting. Handsome.
Tammy
Dreamy. Shy.
Me
Dazed. Confused.

Create a character by writing a page of interior monologue.

Describe a person by what might be written on their gravestone. I'd like mine to say 'She was fun and she never wanted a mobile phone.'

Make up a t-shirt slogan that says it all about someone.

Describe someone by the contents of their room/shed/fridge/handbag. Show the character in action. Describe how they do something, such as cook, chop wood, shop or garden.

Can you create a character in one punchy sentence? The following is a good example. 'Shona is the sort of person who didn't like Bali because it was too dirty.' (Can you imagine her house? No shoes are allowed inside. Everything is pink and beige. Not a pillow is out of place. Your plate is tidied away before you have swallowed the last bite.)

Describe someone in three words. This is William Macey on his wife, Felicity Huffman. 'Generous, lost and late.'

Create a character by blending two people you know. Then give your creation at least two attributes neither of the original people had, but which fit your amalgamated character well.

A character's actions must be in tune with their feelings. **Write a scene** in which the reader can name the emotion by reading about the way a character is doing something.

Oscar Wilde once said, 'It is absurd to divide people into good and bad. People are either charming or tedious.' He also said that if one was invited to dinner, it was one's duty to be entertaining. Write a dialogue between two people at a dinner party that shows one of the characters as charming and the other as tedious.

'I don't own a cell phone or pager. I just hang around everyone I know, all the time. If someone wants to get ahold of me, they just say "Mitch" and I say "what?" and turn my head slightly.' This is a quote by Mitch Hedberg, an American comedian who died at age 37. Based on this, write a day in his life.

Everyone has something to conceal. Raymond Chandler.

Write a short story based on three characters, each of whom is concealing something.

Plot

*The cat sat on the mat. No story. The cat sat on the
dog's mat. Story.* Anon

*The king died and then the queen died. Story. The king
died and then the queen died of grief. Plot.* E. M. Forster

*Often I'll find clues to where the story might go by
figuring where the characters would rather not go.*
Doug Lawson

*Don't say the old lady screamed – bring her on and let
her scream.* Mark Twain

Plot is the backbone of a story. It's a series of events that
drive the narrative along; an arrangement of scenes and
actions which convey a theme. In longer work there may
also be subplots, or stories in a minor key, which echo and
extend the themes of the main plot. A good plot answers
the question 'what happens next?' and continues to do
so, taking the reader on a satisfying journey, without any
boring bits. Novelist Myra Goldberg says, 'Experiment with
structure all you want, but don't forget to tell a story.'

It is said that there are a limited number of basic plots: the love story, the quest, etc. All writers borrow plots, but you will need to make them your own. Make them better, or different. Subvert them, make them funny, make them magical…take them somewhere they have never been before.

Your characters have to want things

Conflict and tension are key elements in plotting. Your characters must experience problems and face adversity. In the first part of a story it's usual to set the scene and introduce your characters. Once the initial scenario is created, you need to give your characters problems, hurdles, unmet needs. Tension and conflict will engross your reader and make them want to read on. Not all conflicts must be major, but they must be meaningful. Conflict may be internal, or between characters. Sometimes there is a series of escalating crises, building to a major crisis. Problems can appear to be solved, only for a new one to arise. By the end of the story or novel, a conclusion must be reached, but be careful not to solve things too early or too neatly.

There is a rise and fall in stories, an internal rhythm. Good writing has a shape, an arc, a satisfying architecture in which all the parts feel right. Even in experimental writing, not built on an obvious beginning, middle and an end, the finished work must feel right. Sometimes you will intuitively know that a piece of writing is working, and sometimes you will know that it isn't working but not be able to sense why.

Make a storyboard. If you are having problems with the order of things, or seeing the shape of the story, you may find storyboarding useful. This is a filmmaking technique whereby you represent the text visually and reduce your story to a series of frames, like a comic strip. In each frame, write what happens in that scene. You can then move frames around, as well as adding or removing them. It's fun, and can bring freshness and fluidity, along with insight about the sequence of events, for example, where the dramatic highlights occur and whether any bits are superfluous. You can also play around with your time frame and subplots. This method can help your fiction become a lot punchier and crisper.

Different authors have different ways of working with plot. Some plan thoroughly first, others let the plot unfold as they go. Lloyd Jones finds writing to be 'an act of discovery, an exercise in discovery. It is not like you sit down with a nice, neatly sequenced plot. The story is a bit of push and pull. You start off laying down the conditions and providing the situation and at some point it picks up some steam and just drags you off into an area you were not expecting. When that happens it is perfect.' Michael Ondaatje speaks of 'an avoidance of plot', and yet in his writing he successfully shifts viewpoints and time frames in a creative layering of material. Raymond Chandler wrote that 'plot is an organic thing' and stated that being committed to a particular pattern before writing appalled him.

Other authors plot intensively beforehand, and create a clear map of their direction before commencing work. Crime writer Elizabeth George says she would never dare begin a book without extensive plotting. In her genre, this makes sense.

Perhaps it is good to consider plotting as being like travel. It is wise to begin with a plan, a map, a loose outline of the journey, but be prepared to change it as you travel. Leave room for the serendipity of new ideas, and know that creative bursts of imagination and brilliance may arrive at any time.

'Plot springs from character,' says writer Anne Lamott. Not everyone agrees with this. Aristotle said that in a good drama, plot is the first essential and that character comes second. It's like the chicken and the egg. Neither comes first. In the best writing plot and character are so well integrated that both are integral to the text, and neither suffers at the expense of the other. Character and story, working together in harmony and balance.

Don't forget, though, that a good plot is one where the actions of the characters feel believable. Be true to your characters and let the story unfold. If you get stuck with a story, be spacious with it. Let the story, the characters and the ideas ferment awhile. Brainstorm, mind map, go walking. Trust in emergence. Often life steps in and as you go about your business, your subconscious has a new bright thought, or you overhear a scrap of dialogue or read something that provides the missing piece in your plot puzzle.

Time

An important thing to be aware of when plotting, which I was taught in a workshop by novelist Owen Marshall, is the relationship between real time and fictional time. Writers manipulate time in various ways. Sometimes they accelerate fictional time so that the reader feels they are in real time. At other times they slow down real time in order to accentuate something. This technique is common in movies. For example, in the final shooting scene in *Bonnie and Clyde* the action slows to highlight the horror of the bloodbath. Owen gave the literary example of Marcel Proust devoting a page to describe a leaf falling. The ability to manipulate time is a valuable tool to have in your writer's repertoire.

Another decision regarding time and plotting is whether to make time linear, eg, to begin at the beginning and continue through the middle until you reach the end, or whether to move around in time, by using flashbacks and other devices.

It is also important to make sure the story begins in the right place. A common mistake for new writers is to over-explain or over-tell the first bit. Experiment by cutting the first few pages or paragraphs of a story. Diving right into the plot can make the work stronger and more exciting.

Good plot questions

- What is the story about? What is the theme?

- Is everything you've written there for a reason?

- Is what happens believable, within the world you have created? Are the actions congruent for your characters?

- Are there any plot threads unresolved?

- Are there too many coincidences?

- Does the story begin in the right place?

- Does the piece feel shapely?

- Do you have a strong plot, or a mere idea? (An idea is a good place to begin, but a story is more than an idea. Plot needs a theme to hold it together.)

- Does the piece have a sense of direction?

- Is it more than a series of episodes?

- Does it need fleshing out, or cutting?

- Is there anything that feels wrong or out of place?

Plot – a handy guide:
Conflict/complications/crisis/resolution.

Exercises

* Create some miniature plot scenarios, such as 'the cat sat on the mat' example, or this one from Graeme Kinross Smith: *I am going to borrow your car. (No story.) Over my dead body! (Story.)*

* Take a short story you have enjoyed reading and storyboard it.

* Take a short story or novel you *hated* and storyboard it.

Form

Every piece of work has the potential to take a variety of shapes. It's important to find the right form for what you have to say. Sometimes it will be immediately obvious what the form should be. A poem will emerge as a poem, an idea will present itself and you will know that is perfect for a short story, or the teacher will demand that you write three haiku. In that situation, just go with it. At other times the best form may prove elusive. Experimentation is the key here. If you try something one way and it doesn't seem to gel, try it another way.

Here are some possibilities for form. The range is huge. Have fun and be creative with your quest for the best form.

- Autobiography. Memoir. Song. Poem (long, short, rhymed?).

- Prayer (See Michael Leunig's wonderful book, *A Common Prayer*).

- Short story. Short short short story. A collection of linked short stories.

- Novel. Novella. Anthology.

- Play. Radio Play.

- Cartoon. Comic strip. Graphic Novel.

- Newspaper article. Magazine article. Blog.

- Dramatic Monologue. Performance Poetry.

- Puppet show. Poster. T-shirt slogan.

- Essay. Travel writing.

- Fairy tale. Myth.

One of the most exciting things that is happening to writing today is that forms are changing all the time. The lines are getting blurred between different forms and genres – between poetry and prose, between poetry and music, between fiction and non fiction. It's an exciting time to be a writer. I encourage you to experiment with form, and to be creative in the forms you attempt. Author Rick Moody says, 'I frankly think that whenever a form looks exhausted that's exactly the point at which you should swoop in and pry it apart and see what makes it tick.'

Sometimes a writer will use the same material in different ways. The following is an example of a poem and a short story, by Alison Georgeson, both of which were inspired by life with her unusual father. Which one do you prefer?

Rewinding Eddie

A smalltime conman, soft-peddling the edges of
the straight and narrow
a widower with two girls and a low tolerance for
frustration, who could always find the perfect
pear; Arcadian romancer who loved the sea.
Standing on a headland
he scanned the jetties
for his windjammer, his sloop, his errant dream boat.

Eddie

Eddie's the type of person who'll wash all your
windows and get his fingers smashed while he's
at it. He'll zoom into town, do your windows and
hightail it back out in a frenzy of perpetual
motion. It's so I can't enjoy my clean windows.
It's to say look how nice and caring I am when
I haven't seen him for seven months and he's
my father. Nine letters to dear daddy came
back addressee unknown and I was fourteen,
living with my sister in an upstairs flat on Derby
Street. No car, no washing machine, no extras:
playing happy families without the parents.
   I sit on the verandah eating fruit and feta,
staring out to sea. It wasn't his fault he was so
irresponsible. Endless stories surround him, each
advancing and surpassing the rest, a crescendo

of bursting colour. In the cool velvet evening his face appears as a cloud that drifts casually towards the horizon.

A smalltime conman, he had his strengths. But he couldn't stay on the straight and narrow; a widower stuck with two girls, a low tolerance for frustration. He would concoct the most elaborate meals, and could always find the perfect pear. He wasn't lazy or callous, just a dreamer. Loved the sea. Standing on a headland, he'd scan the jetties for his dream boat, his sloop, his errant windjammer.

The day Eddie smashed his fingers in my living room window the sun was shining, the freesias were out, there was a soft breeze – a beautiful day. I wanted to sail the boat up the coast, take a picnic, some wine, a sharp cheese and some bread. A game of Mahjong, a lazy afternoon. It would be a sort of reunion-cum-forgiveness ceremony; a few hours to share before he moved on.

Instead, I phoned the doctor. We sped over to his office where Eddie sank into a big soft chair in the waiting room. The pain was easing. It wasn't long before he related his tale to the man on his right. Two minutes into it I heard the first embellishments, and my heart sank; but hey, why can't I just leave him to it?

I rest my head on the back of the chair and close my eyes. There is a tropical shore in the distance, and I swim toward it through warm, clear green water. Gliding onto the beach, I rest my cheek on the hot flat sand as the sun beats down and the waves lap up behind me.

Exercises

Take an incident from your life. Try writing it as a poem, and then as a short short story. Which feels more satisfying?

Write something in a form you have never tried before.

Combine two forms that you don't think have ever been combined before.

Go to your nearest independent bookstore and browse. Check out all the different sections of the shop: sport, poetry, art, cooking, fiction, children's books. What forms are popular? Did any of the books surprise you? You may find that you are inspired by what you see to investigate some new forms yourself.

Place and landscape

Writing is always set somewhere. Whether it's in a messy bedroom or a space pod in the 26th century, your writing will be set in a particular location, and your job as a writer is to bring this place alive for the reader.

Sensory details are a good place to begin when setting the scene. What does it smell like in the noodle bar? What does the laksa taste like? What can you hear: the chink of cutlery, the waitress fumbling with an order, the clang of the till? This sort of information is invaluable; it gives the reader a bridge to cross into the world of the imagination, using their own sense memories.

Landscape is often used as metaphor in literature. Using the physical landscape to echo the emotional one can be a cliché. One of the most overworked and obvious examples is when a character is crying and it's raining: 'Her tears slid down her face as the soft rain dripped down the window.' How boring! However, if you can begin to look at nature in symbolic terms, it's a valuable device. Mountains, highways, rivers, rocks, etc, can all be given symbolic meaning and can provide a writer with juicy material to use in their fiction.

Exercises

❊ My room. My house. My street. My town. My country. My planet. Write a paragraph on each. How can you bring your world to the reader, using simple language yet describing each place in a way that feels fresh and new?

The past is another country. They do things differently there.
L.P. Hartley

❧ Write a page about a place that no longer exists. A small town as it was fifty years ago. The bach or shack you stayed in when you were a kid, which was knocked down to make a waterside palace for some rich guy.

Home is the place where, when you have to go there, They have to take you in.
Robert Frost

❧ Write about a character who is trying to find their way home.

It was as hot as the inside of a baker's oven on a June night in New Orleans.
Jack Kerouac

❧ Invent some similes and metaphors that involve places.

Memphis ain't a bad place, for them that like city life.
William Faulkner

❧ Do you like city life? Or do you prefer the country? Write a piece explaining why.

Gathering Words

Enhancing your vocabulary by collecting words that belong to places will bring a richness and texture to your work.

* The language of geography: mountain, rock, stone, island, ravine

* The language of sky: lightning, star, cloud, rain, horizon, moon

* The language of architecture: hearth, window, roof, hovel, palace, verandah

* The language of interiors: curtain, cobweb, corner, sofa, dust

* The language of journeys: highway, neon, roadside, café

* The language of botany: flax, flower, root, blossom, petal, bud, seed, leaf, thorn

* The language of water: river, snow, ice, creek, puddle, melt, ocean, storm

* The language of flying things: bee, dragonfly, kite, parrot, eagle, moth

Go to the library and borrow some books on a foreign land – one that interests you. Get photography books, maps, Lonely Planet guides, personal accounts.

Write a short story set in this place. Then write a short story set somewhere you know well. Which of these two exercises worked best for you?

Some writers find writing about familiar places is juicy for them, while others work best when taking imaginary places and bringing them to life on the page.

Love at first sight

They told me to expect
the polka dots of sheep
that blew away as the plane came in to land
and they said there'd be
outside dunnies
earthquakes
attitudes that went out with the ark
and a moon that waxed and waned
the Other Way

But no-one told me of
the Kodak blue
the light that made my forehead ache
the rumpled bedsheet of the country's spine
and the brown muscle of Tahuna hills

Nor warned me I was coming home

This wonderful poem by Bridget Auchmuty-Musters was written in response to arriving in Nelson, New Zealand, for the first time. Born in Britain, and well travelled, she liked Nelson so much she settled here. There are places a person immediately feels an affinity with. There are other places – a house, a street, a city or a country – where one immediately feels uncomfortable, or even finds disturbing. Write a piece in which each of these situations becomes apparent. Try this in the first person, as well as the third. Experiment with each point of view, seeing which works best.

Point of view

Every story or poem is told from someone's point of view. One of the first choices you need to make when creating a story or a poem is deciding who is telling the story. Is it told through the eyes of one character? A variety of characters? An all-seeing, all-knowing omniscient narrator? A combination of all of the above?

It's good to experiment when seeking the right perspective. It can be also be daunting and confusing, because each point of view has its own strengths and weaknesses. Sometimes trial and error is the best way to find which will be the most suitable.

First person

If you write in the first person and the 'I' is you, then the work is known as autobiographical. This is the common way of writing family history and memoirs. Here's an example: 'I was born in Auckland, in 1953. My father was a printer. My mother should have been a poet but instead she had babies.'

If you're writing in the first person and it's not about you, it's called creating a persona. Whether the persona is an old man, a toddler eating a peanut butter sandwich, or a sixteen-foot giraffe who loves to tango, you write as if you *are* that person. At its best, this method is fresh, potent, and immediate. The reader stands in the character's shoes and sees the world through their eyes.

First person is a popular choice, and it's a method that flows easily for many writers. However, writing in the first person also has pitfalls. It can be hard to sustain in an interesting way, especially in a longer work. Also, you can't reveal things to the reader that your character doesn't know, which can be limiting, in terms of what it is vital for the reader to know.

Here's an example of first person, in the persona of the main character in *With Lots of Love from Georgia*.

My name is Georgia. I live in a town called Anywhere that has too many shopping malls and not enough skate parks. I'm taller than most fifteen year old girls and I weigh more too. I have wavy red hair that does what it pleases, and my eyes change colour in different lights, from hazelnut to tawny green. I like to think of myself as a brilliant creative person, but sometimes I just feel like a sad lonely girl with a big bum.

I enjoyed writing in Georgia's point of view, and I varied the text with lists, to break up the first person point of view. Something to watch out for is that if your character is an unsympathetic one, not readily likeable, the reader may be alienated. Most people liked *With Lots of Love from Georgia* because they enjoyed seeing the world through the eyes of a lumpy, grumpy cynical girl, but one reader told me that she found Georgia whingey, which meant that there was no way the book was going to work for her.

There's another thing to be careful of when you choose to write using the first person. As many writers use their own lives, thinly disguised as fiction, it's a good idea to make it clear whether you're really writing autobiographical material or fiction. For example, if you submit a story to the school magazine, written in the first person, in which the character sounds much like you and has a sister with a drug problem, readers may well assume that your sister has a drug problem. This is not a good idea, especially if she's a clean-living gal who's trying to get into the police force.

Second person

Second person is not commonly used as a point of view. It's indicated by the word 'you'. Second person is very difficult to sustain. It can work well for small passages, but is rarely used for entire works because it soon begins to feel forced and wooden. The 'you' being addressed may be the reader, or some other character, or God, or even the narrator talking to themselves.

'You think I'm making this up, don't you?' (to the reader)

'Why have you deserted me, Lord?' (to God)

'I suppose you think I'm crazy? You never liked me, right from the start, did you?' (to another character)

You are making a total mess of your life, Logan. You always have and you always will. (character talking to himself)

Third person

Third person is widely used in literature, especially in novels. It's indicated by the use of 'he' or 'she'. Third person can feel more removed than first person, but if executed with finesse, it provides an intimate picture of the characters.

'Marcia was sixteen, going on seven. She knew everything about everything. Well, actually she only thought she did. Marcia actually knew a little about nothing much.'

The most common form of third person is omniscient narration, which means the story is told as if by God, or a big eye-in-the-sky who sees and knows everything. It's a useful perspective because it permits a huge amount of variety. As this narrator, you can skip around in time and space, or amongst your characters at will. You can make lots of complicated plot twists and structural moves, because you know things that the individual characters do not. Think of it as making a movie, where you are the director, producer and scriptwriter combined. When Sam Field and I co-authored *Spacecamp,* we chose omniscient narration because it gave us the scope we needed to create a fictional world, a number of characters and many points of view. Here is an example showing how the narrator can see inside the characters:

'Anyone fancy a bit of nightboarding?' Trey asked hopefully. He felt as if he was interrupting something, although he wasn't sure what. ZZ, Roxy and Silas, had been staring intently at each other for ages. Roxy had never been so happy to have a path-exchange interrupted in her entire fourteen and three-quarter years.'

Point of view

Point of view gives you a huge palette of choices in your writing. Michael Kimball's *How Much of Us There Was* is a good example of an author using a variety of points of view. Some parts are written in the fictional voice of his beloved grandfather, other sections are written in Kimball's own voice. Check it out.

Be brave and have fun experimenting with point of view. Combining first and third person can work well. How about omniscient narration with forays into the first person? If one style feels wrong, try another one. The following exercise may help you explore point of view.

Exercises

Take out your favourite books. Dip into them, taking notice of which point of view they are written in.

Experiment with whose eyes are seeing a story. **Write a scene at a dinner table,** written by various characters at the meal, in which each one has a different version of what happened.

Write about a situation through the eyes of someone who is very old, an overwhelmed shop assistant, a new immigrant, a kid on their first day at school.

Here is a passage from *With Lots of Love from Georgia*, written in the first person. Rewrite it in the third person. Which version do you like best? Why?

'I look like a gothic whale in my black jeans and black shirt. Mum's chunky crystal necklace only serves to make me resemble a whale with good taste in jewellery. By the time I get to Video World it's five o'clock, and I'm all sweaty. When I remove my helmet my hair's stuck to my forehead. I lock my bike out of sight, on the far side of the car park, and lurk around for ages, trying to psyche myself into entering the store. Quite a few customers are coming and going, which strikes me as sad. Surely there are better things to do on a sunny summer's afternoon than watch Arnold Schwarzenegger kick arse, especially as it's the first day of a new year.

"What's the worst thing that can happen?" I ask myself.'

The following poem by writer and Zen teacher Mary Jaksch, is written from the point of view of a mother.

Little Red Car

He waved to me
as he was getting on the plane
lifting his skateboard high,
in his luggage
the little red playmobil car
for his new sister.

At the big old house
he used to play with it
in his room half-way up the landing,
pushing it over the blue vinyl
with gold flecks.
He was little then
and liked to crawl into my bed
at night.

When I pushed him out of my body
and gathered him to my heart
all wet and tiny,
no-one told me
he would become a man
the very next day.

Write a poem inspired by 'Little Red Car' using the point of view of a parent writing about their child. Try reversing the situation and write a poem through the eyes of the boy getting on the plane.

Here is a poem of mine written in the third person. Try rewriting it in the first person. Which do you prefer? Why?

Wonderful Girl

She
loved flowers kisses glances moments
lost her heart and found it a hundred times or more
she wasted nothing
rewrote her history endlessly better every time

She got busy
cleaned the sky washed the clouds polished the
    children
had a cup of tea and then repainted all the many
    worlds

She
spent whole eras in a frenzy of ripe passion
would not curtsy
stepped lightly laughed madly met someone at
    midnight
could not be silenced

She travelled widely
hugged landscapes   studied languages   told secrets
wriggled her ears and ran off with gypsies
           threw the moon across the sky

She
haunted the letterbox   hogged the telephone
   ate what she liked
said what she thought
      and paid whatever the price turned out to be
She never ceased to amaze
just kept on loving flowers   kisses   moments
making choices facing up to life and death

She
got old and died and then got born again again again
She

        is anyone you want the name to be

NB If you're interested in finding out more about point of view, use Google and search for 'writing in the second person'. Many great sites will appear. I suggest you check out the BBC site 'Get Writing A3100104'. I bet you find it extremely helpful. I did.

Dialogue

The world comes to us in stories. One of the most
powerful tools a writer has to create story is the use of
dialogue. Speech is the primary way we communicate
with each other, so being keenly interested in people and
fascinated by the things they say and the way they say them
is a key component of being a juicy writer.

Having an ear for dialogue is both a talent and a skill.
Some writers are naturally gifted in this area, others less so.
If writing dialogue comes easily to you, you're lucky but if
not, it's a skill that can be honed and polished.

When I studied writing at Curtin University, writer
and lecturer Ross Bennett provided us with a list called the
Glasgow Rules. They were devised by a scriptwriter named
Alex Glasgow, and were designed to give the illusion of
'naturalistic' dialogue. Naturalistic, in this context, means
that the dialogue sounds natural, but that all the boring bits
have been cut out so that the essence is preserved. The speech
feels authentic, even though the writer has crafted it by
removing repetitions, umms and ahhs, and other dreary bits
that would drag the work down. I've found these guidelines
invaluable, and hope no one minds if I share them with you.

The Glasgow Rules

1. No more than nine words per utterance.

2. Lots of incomplete sentence fragments.

3. Lots of ellipses, or points of suspension, shown by…

4. Plenty of interruptions, either by the speaker or the other person.

5. Give each speaker a different rhythm or pattern of phrasing.

Also, and most importantly, dialogue must be 'packed'. Packed dialogue means that the things your characters say can't be just waffle. They have to have a reason to be there. So, the second part of the Glasgow Rules goes like this. Each utterance will show or imply:

a. Something about the speaker

b. Something about the person spoken to

c. Something about the situation, eg, the when, how or what

d. Something about the location, eg, where

e. Something about the motivation, eg, why

To sum up, dialogue is a structured and selected version of conversation which gives the illusion of natural speech, while at the same time performing a variety of important functions, such as character development, moving the narrative along, and providing information, either implicit or explicit. Dialogue creates character. It reveals people by the things they say. It's a great tool for creating conflict and tension between your characters, which in turn gives your story the necessary grit.

When creating dialogue, make sure that the words fit the person speaking. It can be useful to give some of the characters particular speech patterns, but be careful not to overdo the stutter, the slang or whatever idiosyncrasy you give the speaker. A light hand is far more effective than a heavy one.

It's also wise to avoid using dialogue for clumsy plot advances, or retells. Examples of this 'no-no' are common in the scripts of daytime television dramas. For example: 'Yesterday I saw Jane and Harold who've just had twins and gone to live in Mexico because they fell out with their neighbours the day after Harvey got sacked from his job at the film studio for sleeping with his secretary.'

There are several ways dialogue can be presented. The first way is to use speech (quotation) marks.

'Bring me my wallet, Jake. It's on the table.'

'I can't see it.'

'Try my coat pocket then.'

Sometimes dialogue is presented without speech (quotation) marks.

- Bring me my wallet, dude. It's on the table.

- Can't see it, bro.

- Look under the bed, just in case.

Sometimes an exchange occurs within a paragraph:
I wish you'd bring me my wallet, Ben says. Bossy is my brother's middle name. Can't find it, I reply. If I stall him long enough, he'll get annoyed and look for it himself.

When writing dialogue, try to make it clear who's saying what with the minimum of 'he saids' and 'she saids'. Often the context will make it clear who's speaking but sometimes you can keep the reader on track by following the line of dialogue with an action or thought by the speaker.

> 'I can't come out tonight.' Marcy scowled at herself in the mirror, her cold sore scowling back at her.

> 'Be home by midnight, or else.' My mother lit another cigarette.

Keep fancy tag lines, such as 'she whispered' and 'he snarled' to a minimum. Amateur writers often go overboard with these. You have been warned!

Here's a dialogue excerpt from *The Transformation of Minna Hargreaves* by Fleur Beale. You'll see that the author has used dialogue to good effect, developing the characters and moving the story along at a cracking pace. Note that she helps the reader keep track of who's speaking to whom, by using names within some of the lines spoken. The interior dialogue of Minna, the protagonist, gives the passage texture, as does the fact that dialogue is skilfully placed amongst details of the meal. Also note that sometimes the fact that someone is *not* speaking is significant, as are the character's actions during the scene.

We finished, and I hadn't said anything the whole entire meal. Mum asked a couple of polite questions and Dad babbled on about the stupid island and how even if we didn't go, he'd arranged to spend a couple of weeks there by himself and wasn't that awesome?

Mum put down the slice of pizza she'd nibbled. I wish she wouldn't do that — eat it or leave it is my motto. She spoke to Dad, not to me, 'We'll do it, Wes. We'll all go to the island. For the year.'

I choked and spluttered, but thank goodness I had Lizzie. Dad whooped and hollered and carried on like we'd won the biggest lottery in the universe.

'But Mum — why?' I couldn't believe she was actually agreeing. 'You don't want to do it! Look at you! You look as if you're going to prison — you're crazy.'

She didn't respond to that, and Dad didn't pick up on it either, I was interested to note. Instead, Mum said, 'You might like to take a look at your son.' She told him the Noah story, but left out the chapter titled Rescue by Minna.

Dad shot out of the room, came back, sat down, didn't say anything.

I stood up. 'Well, you lot can go and play happy families on the island. Not me. I'm staying with Lizzie.'

Mum did look at me then. 'No, Minna. You're not. You're coming too. We're a family. We're staying together and we're all going.'

Exercises

Take a notebook to town. Sit in a café or the railway station, visit the supermarket or the library. Make an art form of eavesdropping. Listen to people and record the things they say. Collect fragments of dialogue, odd speech habits, one-liners, interchanges that intrigue. Make this a daily practice, so that listening is a skill you are constantly developing.

Take notice of dialogue when you read. By analysing the way other writers use dialogue, you'll learn a lot.

Write a dialogue between two people that shows they completely misunderstand each other.

Write a dialogue in which one person shows the other that they love them, without using the words 'I love you.'

Rework the two dialogues above by setting them somewhere. Are your characters in a car, a laundromat, on a sofa watching rugby? It's important not to just have talking heads. Inserting chunks of dialogue will feel clunky if it's not given a location.

'My senior moments seem to have all fused together.' The elderly woman who said this was a joyous creative spirit with a sharp intelligence and a wicked sense of humour. **Write an interior monologue** for this woman, showing her character.

Recently I was in a funky shop called Tula and Niles, crowded with art deco vases, antique handbags, old Hawaiian shirts, fabulous dresses and unusual earrings. I was buying earrings when I overheard Christie, the proprietor, say this: 'I prefer living in the fullness of the ever-unfolding moment.'

Create a dialogue between Christie and a customer in her shop in which it becomes clear that Christie's more of a philosopher than your average salesperson.

Jake's seventeen. He's a vegetarian who believes in green politics. He says he enjoys surprising people and knowing what to do, but that the world intervenes and neither happens all that often.

Write a dialogue between Jake and another character that illustrates Jake's quirky character. Is the other character like-minded? Or definitely not?

Use these dialogue fragments to inspire a piece of writing.

'I just wish she would grow up and be fabulous again, sigh.'

'I despise summer. I prefer dark weather.'

'For my sake, don't buy that car.'

'Oh well, keep smiling is my motto now, as time ebbs away…'

Why you have to make your characters miserable

Good books don't give up all their secrets at once.

Stephen King

If the characters are having a good time, the reader isn't.

Jerry Cleaver

In order to make story, there has to be what is called narrative tension, or narrative drive. Story is created when things happen. If nothing happens, there's no story. 'I got up, had a piece of toast, then had another piece of toast, then looked out the window for awhile, then went and fed my turtle. Then I listened to the radio, with the sound turned down.' Sorry, you don't have a story, and your reader is asleep.

In order to engage your reader, you have to invite them in. First lines are important. So are first paragraphs and first pages. Your task is to set up a time and a place and some interesting protagonists.

Here is a beautiful beginning by Kate Duignan, to a piece of short fiction titled 'Stories We Tell About Our Sister'.

> For twelve days and nights we call her Tuppence. Before Christmas there is snow and a fox crosses the garden. A name falls on her head like a star.

I like this beginning because it has a sense of mystery. I want to know more. Who is Tuppence? What happened after the twelve days and nights?

After inviting your reader in, things have to happen. And more things. These conflicts and actions need to shift the characters, so that by the end of the story something has changed, both in circumstance and in the inner world of the character. There need to be obstacles, which are overcome. But not too easily. Life is messy, and to be authentic that messiness has to be in the story.

Jerry Cleaver puts it this way. He says that Want and Obstacle = Conflict. He suggests you ask these two vital questions of your story. Who wants what? What is the obstacle? Bear in mind that the *want* must be very important to the character. It might be something as small as wanting to stay up late and watch TV, but if the show in question is the character's absolute favourite, and if they are already having issues with their mother, an interaction over this particular desire can be powerful.

An obstacle and the way it is handled must also reveal something about character, for the story to contain meaning. For example, a boy is walking along the road.

He's fifteen. He's wearing baggy jeans, a ripped black t-shirt and bare feet. As he passes the deli on the corner, a younger kid, a freckly dude about thirteen, throws an empty soft drink can, meaning it to land in the nearby bin. He misses. The can bounces off the edge of the overflowing rubbish bin and hits the passing boy. Unfortunately, the can isn't quite empty, so sticky soft drink goes all over the bottom of his jeans and his feet. The younger boy mumbles an apology. 'Sorry, man.' What does the older boy do? Thump the younger guy in the teeth? Grin and walk on? Give a mean look? Or snarl and give the finger? The response shows the reader a lot about his character.

There is a third component to creating story. There must be conflict and action, and finally there must be resolution. Not all resolution has to be sewn up tightly. Sometimes a hint of mystery and ambiguity can work well. Nevertheless, the reader must be left satisfied. Ending a story is a delicate operation. If it is left too ambiguous and open-ended your reader will be frustrated and disappointed. If you tie your ending up too tightly, the reader will feel as if the message has been rammed down their throat.

Exercises

Write some beginnings. Imagine you are starting the first page of a novel. How will you invite the reader in? By the end of the first page, you will need to have created a world that has meaning, a tone, a voice, and maybe a hint of a problem.

Problems and solutions

Write a scene in which there are two characters. Create a problem. Write three possible scenarios, each one providing a different direction for the story.

Go to the library. Check out the beginnings and endings of some contemporary novels. Notice which ones work for you, and why. Notice any devices that inspire your creativity, and any that feel particularly lame.

Exposition, development, drama

Frank O'Connor says in *The Lonely Voice* that there are three necessary elements in a story: exposition, development and drama. Exposition we may illustrate as 'John Fortescue was a solicitor in the little town of X'; development as 'One day Mrs Fortescue told him she was about to leave him for another man'; and drama as '"You will do nothing of the kind," he said.'

Take the above example, and illustrate it with three sentences of your own.

Polishing the diamond

A sentence should contain no unnecessary words.
    The Elements of Style by William Strunk and E.B. White

Things should be made as simple as possible, but not any simpler.   Albert Einstein

The ability to simplify means to eliminate the unnecessary so that the necessary may speak.
                    Hans Hofmann, painter

Substitute damn every time you're inclined to write very; your editor will delete it and the writing will be just as it should be.   Mark Twain

Ernest Hemingway famously said that the first draft was always rubbish, although he actually put it more rudely than that. However, the final draft has to be good. It can be a long journey between those two points. Every journey is different but guidelines can be useful.

The first draft
The first task is to produce some material. This sounds

easy but sometimes getting started is tricky. If you want to be brilliant straight up, it's hard to even start. The inner critic, that voice that says you are dumb as soon as you attempt something, can be crippling. If this helps, try imagining this negative force as an actual creature: such as a black monkey or a hawk with a sharp destructive beak. Once you have visualised your punishing critic, send it away to a suitably gruesome end. Your creative spirit needs friends, not enemies.

Now you have total permission to play. Let the words and ideas flow freely, without worrying about correct spelling, punctuation, tidiness or logic. First draft is a place for fun, creativity, silliness, imagination, irrational thoughts, wonderment and pleasure. Be fast and loose, or slow and dreamy. Don't worry if the material comes out higgledy piggledy, just let it be. Later on, this juicy material can be revised, edited, corrected and improved.

Editing

Editing is a special process of its own. Once you have the bones of something it's time to bring in your critical faculty, only this time in its kindest gentlest guise. Again, if visualisation works well for you, imagine your 'editor mind' as a wise scholarly aunt or uncle, or a sharp snazzy pen that knows everything. It can work well to let first draft material sit for a while before you edit it, so you come to it with a fresh eye, but at other times it will feel right to attack it right away.

I find colourful highlighters or coloured pencils useful at this point.

Start by reading the work aloud. Choose a suitable colour and highlight any word, phrase or paragraph that feels wrong, even if you aren't quite sure why it's jarring or how to fix it. Look out for clumsy rhythms, dull patches, or places where you've used the same word or idea twice.

Aim for quality not quantity

One very common flaw is repeating the same thing in different wording, hereby to be known as waffling. Many of us were taught as small children that writing a lot was a good idea. If you could write pages and pages for a school assignment and if you didn't make many spelling mistakes, you were likely to get a big tick and a sticker of a daisy or a rainbow. Unfortunately, writing pages and pages of clichés and repetitions doesn't equal good writing. In fact, the kid who stared out the window, the dreamy one who chewed their pencil and only wrote one line, may have been the better writer, if that line was a fabulous line containing an original idea or a fresh way of seeing or saying something. In the best writing not a word is wasted. One of my first writing teachers, the late Penny Brown, put it this way, 'Use every word as if it cost a thousand bucks.'

Clichés

So, pick another colour and use it to highlight clichés. In its simplest form a cliché is a word combination that has been used before. Some examples: a lovely red rose, an evil witch, a nice sunny day. Your challenge as a writer is to find a way to offer the rose, the witch or the day to the reader in an original way. Graeme Kinross-Smith advises, 'Do not use any phrase, statement or word combination if you have the faintest suspicion you might have heard or seen it before.'

If you can't think of anything fresh or juicy, remove the offender and don't replace it. A sentence is always better when it loses saggy over-worked adjectives. Less is more. If the noun is strong and it is doing a good job there is no need for an adjective at all.

An idea or a plot line can also be a cliché. Sometimes we get lazy and use a tired word combination, phrase or idea, but if the reader is going along a predictable path, they will soon get bored. Novelist Martin Amis says, 'All writing is campaign against cliché. Not just clichés of the pen but clichés of the mind and heart.'

Sometimes what you've written feels a bit ploddy. Use a third colour to highlight areas which feel somehow 'less than' and ask yourself 'what's missing?' Perhaps adding a few sensuous details or an original metaphor can enliven the work and make it shine.

Overtelling

Overtelling is another common flaw. As Voltaire famously remarked, the secret of being tiresome is to tell everything. Leave some space for the reader to do some work. Don't labour the point. Trust that your readers are intelligent and will enjoy joining up the dots.

Lazy adverbs

Writer Fleur Beale teaches her students to beware of lazy adverbs. In this example – 'to walk slowly' – the verb is 'walk' and the adverb is 'slowly'. Your task is to do the same job with one strong verb. I came up with the following: dawdle, stroll, saunter, trudge, meander, shuffle, amble, lope. Can you think of any others? Again, there is a better way of saying 'to eat quickly'. Consider using one of these: scoff, pig, guts, gobble, hog, wolf, devour, or stuff.

The ending

Take special notice of your ending. Have you tried to end the story too quickly? Resolving a plot too soon and too glibly is a common mistake. The reader will feel cheated if the story suddenly ends, if there are unbelievable coincidences, or if there are threads left incomplete. Don't even think of ending a story with 'And then I woke up because it was all just a dream.' Maybe the first person who had that idea was clever, but the ninety-seven thousand who came after them were merely lazy.

Extra editing advice

I like editing my work but on a bad day it can feel like a hard task. Sometimes I need to rearrange my brain. I tell myself that I'm fabulous for having done a first draft, and now I am going to be even more fabulous because I'm about to turn my good first draft into a brilliant second draft. With this new attitude, I begin to enjoy myself and add and subtract, polish and embroider, carefully replacing a dodgy adjective with a strong one, or adding a sentence that lifts a story to higher ground. Once I abandon the idea that the task is arduous and greet it as a chance to make good work better, I find the pleasure. So, lavish your work with love and creativity. If you start to feel stale, bored and grumpy, go for a walk in the park, or eat some chocolate, and come back when you feel more zesty.

Sometimes the answers to what needs attention in your writing will come to you at once, sometimes it will take longer. It can be helpful to put the work away and return to it later. It's really important not to neglect this stage. Don't hurry. Or, as the Latin proverb says, *Festina Lente*, which means 'hurry slowly'. If you are keen to 'be done with' a piece of work and send it out into the world before it's ready, you're missing a valuable chance to make your writing the best it can possibly be. If you are really stuck, put the ailing story, song or poem away, for a day, a week or even a month. When the spirit moves you, return to it afresh. It's amazing what you'll see when you read it again with new eyes.

Don't abandon your editing forever though, just because it feels hard. Taking a break can be a good idea, but coming back to the task is also good. It's important to persevere. Sometimes you have to put in the extra effort, and sit down at that chair one more time. Even if you're lonely and bored, even if you'd rather be trawling the mall, there'll be times when you need to apply some bum glue. If you give your work the necessary time and editorial attention it deserves, it will pay off in the long run. There's nothing more depressing than a whole heap of unfinished work. I encourage you to honour your work and your process by bringing it to fruition, at least some of the time.

Feedback

It can be useful to show your work to someone else and ask for feedback. Other people are particularly good at spotting basic things, like punctuation or spelling errors. Do you know the difference between a colon and a semi-colon? A good grammar book or an eagle-eyed English teacher can be useful. Maybe you have a habit of using too many exclamation marks? Remember that 'Thou shalt not commit random acts of senseless punctuation' and edit your work accordingly.

Ray Coffey, the editor of Fremantle Arts Centre Press, said there are two sorts of people who are difficult to work with. The first is the person who won't change a thing because everything they do is already perfect. Obviously, this stubborn person will never learn or improve. However, the other sort of person who's difficult to edit is the one who agrees to every suggestion and hands over all their power to the editor. Don't feel that you must go along with editorial suggestions or changes if they feel destructive or detrimental to your intention. Remember that the work belongs to you, but don't be closed to editorial wisdom and advice. Trust that other people can sometimes see things that you can't. In this way, the editing process will be a dialogue between two intelligences, the aim being to make the work as strong as possible.

One last thought about getting editorial advice. My friend Alison Georgeson told me of a fantastic Japanese saying which goes like this: 'If ten people tell you you're drunk, sit down.' This means that if everyone you show your story to says they don't understand the ending, then you probably need to clarify the ending!

Two small but important editing tips.

Proofread carefully to see if you any words out.

Everyone has a word, or maybe several words, that they overuse. (Mine are quirky, cool, funky, mermaid and fabulous.) Seek out your own overworked words and banish them.

Not just little green men

There is a theory which states that if ever anybody discovers exactly what the Universe is for and why it is here, it will instantly disappear and be replaced by something even more bizarre and inexplicable. There is another theory which states that this has already happened.

Douglas Adams

Science fiction

What do you love reading? It's often what you love writing, too. For many the preferred genre is science fiction, also known as fictional science or speculative fiction. Are you intrigued by the possibilities of future worlds, strange technologies and alien races? No doubt you are already a buff.

Robert A. Heinlein defines the genre this way: 'realistic speculation about possible future events, based solidly on adequate knowledge of the real world, past and present, and on a thorough understanding of the nature and significance of the scientific method.'

In my twenties I read quite a bit of sci-fi. The handsome

young med student I was in love with read Philip K. Dick, so I did too, and I was knocked out by Kurt Vonnegut Jr.'s take on things in *Cat's Cradle*. In this bizarre text Vonnegut created a new religion, Bokononism, and also a new way of mating or 'exchanging awareness', whereby people sat in silence, facing each other, with the soles of their feet touching. Vonnegut also invented a vocabulary, which included these words: wampeter, foma, granfalloon, suprass, duffle, sinook, swoo and the wonderful Zah-mah-ki-bo, which means your fate or inevitable destiny. In *Cat's Cradle* everyone belongs to an invisible tribe, or karass. If you found your life tangled up with somebody else's life for no logical reason, that person was probably a member of your karass. By inventing a whole new language and culture Vonnegut was able to comment on his own culture, many aspects of which he found absurd.

After many years of reading other genres my interest in science fiction was revived when I wrote *Spacecamp* with my son, Sam Field. In *Spacecamp*, life on Earth has become highly technological. People live in climate-controlled domes. They no longer know how to cook and they haven't walked in mud, or seen a hedgehog or a rainbow. A team of gifted teenagers go on a school camp to Phoenixia, a newly discovered planet where they encounter natural phenomena for the first time. They also meet a highly-developed civilization of amazing ants, giant green monsters and an electronic bee that saves the day. As Sam said, the book is mildly ecological, and it was a way we could explore some of our ideas about what will be lost if we continue to destroy the natural resources of the planet.

One of the pleasures of both reading and writing science fiction is that it's immense fun. Brazilian novelist, Doris Fleury says she finds writing sci-fi a joy because 'you can have everything. You can throw in androids, time machines, whatever you want. You have absolute control.' You can't let your book become a 'gypsy donkey' though, which Doris describes as something overloaded, jumbled and crazy. Your imagined reality must be carefully planned and have depth and believable logic. The strange must become real, or real enough that your reader can enter the new world with you. The reader must also care about the characters. As sci-fi author Theodore Sturgeon notes, 'a good science fiction story is a story about human beings, with a human problem, and a human solution.'

Fantasy

Fantasy is another very popular genre. It's not my favourite, although the best is brilliant. If you enjoy fantasy, you'll know that the difference between science fiction and fantasy is that in science fiction the story can't contradict what is currently accepted as scientific fact. It may however speculate on scientific possibilities yet to be discovered. A fantasy story is one in which the conditions are contrary to scientific fact. Magic happens, and supernatural beings can interfere in human affairs.

Remember that whatever genre you choose, the basics of good writing apply. Avoid clichés in your writing and make sure you have intriguing characters, a gripping beginning and a satisfying ending.

Exercises

Go to the library and pick up one of the more accessible, science magazines, like *New Scientist* or *Wired*. Find an article about something that sparks your imagination about one possible future, and write a short story based on it.

Want to know more? Check out Wikipedia on Science Fiction.

Cult TV series *Firefly* cleverly mixes two genres: science fiction and the western, and can probably be found in your local video store, along with the ensuing movie, *Serenity*. These texts are also great examples of character development, the use of humour and sharp dialogue. Check out the quirky swearing. It's not in English, so you can use it freely and not get into trouble at school. Have a shiny time!

Read Douglas Adams and Terry Pratchett, who very successfully mix sci-fi with humour. You may also wish to try Ray Bradbury, Philip K. Dick, Ursula Le Guin and Philip Pullman, or Mary Shelley's Gothic novel *Frankenstein*.

Use one of the following quotes as inspiration for a story.

> *The function of the imagination is not to make strange things settled, so much as to make settled things strange.*
>
> G.K. Chesterton

*In those days spirits were brave, the stakes were high,
men were real men, women were real women and
small furry creatures from Alpha Centauri were real
small furry creatures from Alpha Centauri.*

Douglas Adams

*They began as manufacturers of electronic mood
organs and player pianos. Then they started building
exact simulacra of famous men. They thought that
people would pay a good price to have anyone they
wanted made to order – to talk with or to utilize.
But they ran into trouble. For one thing an exactly
programmed reconstruction of a noted personality is
going to be as obstinate and character/complex as the
real man was – and nobody's puppet.*

cover blurb of *We Can Build You* by Philip K. Dick

*A whirlwind transports a ship sailing beyond the
Pillars of Hercules to the Moon, where the voyagers
find the King is about to go to war with the Emperor of
the Sun over rights to colonize Venus. Fabulous beasts
such as flea archers the size of elephants are employed.*

Lucian 160 A.D. *Vera Historia*

Something to ponder

It can be argued that science fiction plays an important role
in the technological development of our society. Almost
a century before the daring flights of the astronauts, Jules
Verne wrote *From the Earth to the Moon*, in which three

members of a gun club build a rocket that takes them to the moon, from where they return with an ocean landing. Apollo 11 was spookily similar: three astronauts take off from Florida, and return to earth safely by splashing down in the ocean. In his famous *20,000 Leagues Under the Sea*, Verne predicted that fast ocean-going submarines would be used for research and exploration, even though nothing remotely like them had yet been invented. Verne's stories seem eerily close to predicting future events. Do you think writers actually play a part in sparking the imagination of inventors and scientists?

Alternatively, do you think that by dramatically playing out dire consequences, sci-fi writers can stop undesirable futures coming to pass? The late great Ray Bradbury said, 'People ask me to predict the future, when all I want to do is prevent it.'

What is your reason for writing science fiction? Is it a venue for your wildest imaginings or does it have a deeper purpose?

Resources

The following great books are by David Pringle. See the Bibliography for publication details.

- *The Ultimate Guide to Science Fiction: An A–Z Guide to S F Books*
- *The Ultimate Encyclopedia of Fantasy*
- *Imaginary People: A Who's Who of Modern Fictional Characters*

FIVE

WRITING AND LIFE

Let the magic begin

Creativity and healing

Earth laughs in flowers.   Ralph Waldo Emerson,
                        writer and philosopher (1803-1882)

Relax and stay present.   Zen Wisdom

To write the stories of our lives, to give voice to our troubles, our hopes and our shadowy secrets, is a brave and important thing. Novelist Alice Walker said, 'I write to save my own life.' Jeanette Winterson put it this way, 'If you tell yourself as a story it doesn't seem as bad.'

It's common to sneer at writing as 'therapy', and it's true that some writing is best left in the privacy of your diary or journal. A judge in a teen writing competition in New Zealand wryly commented that many of the entries weren't so much short stories as suicide notes. So, writing fifteen pages of sorrowful ramblings about the object of your affection dumping you may or may not make you feel better about things, but it ain't art. Ranting your way through a problem, or getting something off your chest in the form of a scribbled fury or an unsent letter can be very useful to you, but won't necessarily lead to a piece of publishable work.

However, often getting something off your chest can clear an energy block so that the good writing can begin. There may be things you don't want to go public with, but by writing your way through them, you will find that you become more steady and spacious, and your creativity flows more easily. As Rachel Remen wrote in the preface to John Fox's *Poetic Medicine,* 'One of the best kept secrets in this technically oriented culture is that simply speaking the truth heals.' Novelist Rick Moody, who wrote *The Ice Storm* and *Garden State*, says if you 'let creativity flower in your personality' it really helps keep depression at bay. If you have had traumatic events in your life and are struggling with residual emotions, or are having hard times dealing with hard things, journal writing can be a powerful way to untangle your knots. Free write. Give yourself the time and space to write your way through the fear, the anger, the sorrow, or the confusion. Let the feelings out. Don't censor yourself. The white page is a safe place for all your murky bits. When you've finished, feel free to destroy, bury, shred or even to frame the pages. You will feel lighter and ready to move on.

If you face your demons in this way, the energy of strong emotions can lead to very strong writing. Many brilliant love songs or important poems were born from the raw pain of being alive, because the writer was brave enough to first feel and then document the emotion.

Writers use the material of their own lives in many ways. The late Elizabeth Jolley told our writing class at Curtin University that she sometimes documented on an index card, in detailed form, how it felt to be angry, or lonely, when she was right in the midst of it. The next time she was writing an angry or a lonely character, out came the card.

Some writers, such as Augusten Burroughs and David Sedaris, use humour to leaven the lives they've led. Other writers, like Frank McCourt, tell the story straight. His book, *Angela's Ashes*, detailing his early life of poverty and hardship, not only became a bestseller and a movie, it helped McCourt put his past to rest. Strong work will do well, because it acknowledges the important stuff, the deep wounds and the dodgy corners of what it means to be alive.

Nora Ephron was told by her mother that the tragedies of your life have the potential to be comic stories. Ephron is a great example of the philosophy that if you've got lemons, make lemonade. Ephron's parents were alcoholics and she didn't have an easy childhood, but she's been brave enough to use the material of her life in a variety of ways. She's a prize-winning essayist, journalist, novelist and the scriptwriter of a swag of good movies, including *Sleepless in Seattle*, *When Harry Met Sally*, *Silkwood* and *You've Got Mail*.

As well as being a place of healing through dealing with darkness, there's a huge amount of pleasure in being a writer. Writing is an invitation to spirit and the intellect. In the world of words and ideas the qualities of playfulness and creativity are encouraged, unlike the everyday world where at times these qualities are actively discouraged. Diane Ackerman says that writing is her form of celebration and prayer, as well as her form of enquiry.

Many writers feel the same. Writing connects us to who we are, at the deepest level, and to other human beings, to whatever is bigger than all of us – whether they name it God, the Tao, or the great beyond.

Exercises

❖ Mary Oliver says, 'you only have to let your soft body love what it loves.' What do you love? Fear? Long for?

Write a short story in which the main character deals with a strong emotion in an unusual way. Make this the key to your plot.

What could you change in your life that would encourage your creativity, your soul and your spirit to flourish?

The answer to this question will be unique to you. Maybe you're feeling sluggish and disconnected from your body. How about taking up karate, yoga or salsa dancing? Are you feeling dull and boring? Perhaps you need to dress more wildly, get a new haircut, get a heap of travel books out of the library, cut back on watching junk television, learn another language? When my cousin hit hard times she decided to take her little dog, Flopsy, to visit the residents of an old folks' home as part of a cheer-up scheme. Helping other people helped her to move out of her own miseries. By connecting with and helping others, her own life gained meaning and pleasure.

What's all of this got to do with my writing, you may be asking?

Here's the important thing: Your life and your writing are not separate. They are intricately connected in mysterious ways, and adjustments in one will affect the other. Don't take my word for it, experiment for yourself.

If you're interested in this aspect of the creative process, Julia Cameron and Natalie Goldberg are good people to read. Check out their titles in the Juicy Bibliography.

Finish these sentences:

↬ I like…

↬ I love…

↬ I wish…

↬ I remember/don't remember…

↬ I will never…

↬ I used to…but now I…

↬ If I had a magic wand…

↬ If I was God…

Write your life as a fairytale. Myths and legends have tremendous power.

Start with one of the following, or create your own:

Fairytale archetypes

* The Ugly Sister

* The Almost Handsome Prince

* The Wicked Stepmother

* The Magician

* The Shoemaker

* The Warrior

* The Mermaid

* The Sulky Princess

* The Nearly Normal Bridesmaid

Dreamwork

Dreams are messages to ourselves from our deepest wisdom; a wellspring of creativity and knowledge. Dreams can tell us things we need to hear, they can guide us to look at areas in our life and our work that need attention. Many artists, writers and other creative people find that taking notice of their dreams brings them insights and imaginative treasures.

There are many ways to work with dreams to enhance your creativity.

Here's an example. If you have a dark scary dream and wake up feeling awful, write the dream down. Now rewrite the ending so that your dream ends in a positive way instead of a terrifying way. By reclaiming your power, your spirits will lift and your day will feel much more positive. A bad dream can leave you feeling crushed and worried, but taking charge of the narrative can be immensely healing and bring creative energy back into your inner world.

Another healing way to work with dreaming is to use the messages your dreams provide as helpful guides to your creative life. Sarah, a zesty sixteen-year-old, was having nightmares crammed with catastrophic events. She'd wake up feeling overwhelmed and anxious. When she asked herself what the message of the dream was, Sarah realised that she was feeling overwhelmed and anxious in subtle ways during the daytime as well. By cutting down on some of her many extra-curricular activities, Sarah's life became more relaxed and her song-writing began to flow again.

A good book to read if you're interested in using dream work to help your creativity is *Living The Dream: A guide to Working with Your Dreams* by Sally Gillespie.

Affirmations

If you're feeling fragile, challenged and miserable, it's hard to get through the day, let alone be creative. Find some affirming phrases that resonate for you. Pin them up in your writing space. Let them inspire you. Affirmations work for me. They remind me of the joys of the writing life, when I am getting bogged down in the difficulties. Novelist Sue Monk Kidd's screen saver says: Love. Find Joy. Be Present.

Here are some other suggestions:

- ✒ I am creative, wonderful and wise.

- ✒ Let the magic begin.

- ✒ It is safe to be me.

Treat yourself well

Sometimes writers are so busy in their minds, they get stuck in their heads and forget all about their bodies. Similarly, they can get so interested in intellectual matters, that they ignore their feelings.

The twelve step programme of Alcoholics Anonymous has a useful acronym: HALT, which stands for Hungry, Angry, Lonely or Tired. This handy guide serves to remind the person with the addiction to pay particular attention to those four states because when they're in one of them, it's much more likely that their addiction will kick in.

HALT is also a useful acronym for a writer. If you're having any of those four feelings strongly, you need to take notice and stop what you're doing. Often simply having a snooze, or a meal, or a talk with someone, or asking for a hug, can make a real difference to your day, and this will give a boost to your creativity as well. I promise that if you treat yourself like a precious object, not only your health, but also your writing will benefit. Natalie Goldberg says that when she's working on a novel, she makes sure she looks after herself royally, by eating properly, taking naps, getting a good night's sleep, and doing the right amount of socialising. In this way she's able to sustain her creative energy during the long journey of writing a book.

Jungian psychologist Marie-Louise von Franz suggested that one of the most destructive psychological forces is unused creative power. I agree. If you have a creative gift it is incredibly important to use it. If left to wither, creative energy can become destructive energy. Teacher and educator Sylvia Ashton-Warner had a lovely metaphor for this. She described humans as being like two volcanoes: one destructive, one creative. She believed that the more you feed the volcano of creativity, the less powerful your destructive volcano will be. I have found this to be true in my own life. The more I nourish my creativity, the more my creativity nourishes my own well-being. Singers need to sing to be happy, dancers need to dance, and writers need to write. Believe in yourself. Use your gifts and let the magic begin.

> *I vow from now on to be my own best friend first and my harshest critic second.* Ben Mitchell, artist

Honouring who you are

Everything that happens to me goes into the soup and comes out a different way.

Stephen Poliakoff, playwright and TV dramatist

If you want to work on your art, work on your life.

Anton Chekhov

To be a good writer, you have to be yourself. Who else could I possibly be, you may ask, but some people spend their entire lives bending themselves into strange shapes that don't feel right to them. It's not a good idea, for many reasons. Trying to fit into others' expectations brings suffering. In order to be happy, you need to be comfortable in your own skin. It is as simple and as challenging as that.

It's especially important to find out who you are if you want to be a writer. The life you live will feed into your work. If your experiences aren't authentic, then your work will not be authentic either. Great writers have lives, and their work arises from fully realising, or at least grappling with the beauty and pain of their living.

A horse must be a horse and a giraffe must be a giraffe.

A peacock will never be a flamingo. Or to put it another way, Ben Elton has to be Ben Elton, Nick Hornby has to be Nick Hornby and neither of them should spend their life trying to be Matthew Reilley. The sort of person you are will reflect the kind of writer you become. If you are a cynical person who loves popular culture, this will be reflected in your work. Similarly, if you are a dreamy, poetic, whimsical person, you are unlikely to write taut plot-driven detective novels.

It's also important to honour the way your life and your work intertwine, and to explore the conditions that work best to get you into the right space to write. The working day that suits you will depend on the type of person you are. Some people find quiet, steady conditions the best, others work best when there's a bit of pace and edge.

Diane Ackerman, in her essay 'Courting The Muse', tells of all the strange things writers do in order to get themselves in the mood to create. From drinking twenty-five cups of tea a day like diarist Samuel Pepys, or sniffing rotten apples like Schiller, they all had seemingly bizarre routines that helped them write.

I love the following true story. It encourages me to be who I am. When Diane Ackerman asked New York resident and novelist William Gass if he had any strange habits that got him in the mood for writing, he replied that he didn't. When pressed to reveal the details of his daily regime, he said he spent his morning taking photographs of grungy, seedy places in New York, where he lived. Filth and decay, mainly, he told her. Don't you find this strange? Ackerman asked. Not for me, Gass replied.

Not for me. The perfect answer.

Find your own way

Everyone is unique, and the conditions that will support them best will also be individual.

I can relate to William Gass being inspired by dodgy places though, because I also find dusty downtrodden areas of cities absorbing. I'd like to begin my day by wandering the streets of Brooklyn or the East Village, soaking up the street life. Then I would go home and write, fed by the myriad tastes and sights and sounds of life and people in all their messy glory.

However, because I live in a small quiet town in the top of the South Island of New Zealand, my daily routine is very different. It involves beginning my day with meditation. This simple practice, just sitting quietly, allowing the sounds of the day and the aches in my body their place, tunes me in to my heart and mind. It feeds me, grounds me, brings me home to myself. Next, I take a pot of strong tea and some toast back to bed. I also take a pile of books and magazines to read, which I fondly refer to as research. Research, for me, also involves walking, grocery shopping, visiting the library, staring out the window and drawing in my journal. If you watched me, you might think I potter around all day, picking a flower and putting it in a vase, making a phone call, chopping vegetables for soup. However, I've learned over time that this is how I work. I moodle through the day and somehow, sometime, I sit down at my desk and do some writing. I have fed my body, mind and spirit, and taken the day gently. These are the conditions that work best for me.

Every writer has their own way of working. It might involve a laptop and plenty of coffee, it might involve a purple pen, a green notebook and a certain flavour of ice-cream; it might involve being in a library, or writing on the bus. Once you find and accept what works for you, the work will flow easier. Your pattern may change over time, and the delicate act of juggling life with work will be a work-in-progress, or perhaps an unsteady tower of cards that somehow manages to stay in the air. It will also be unique to you.

Helen Garner writes about a writing mentor sending her a postcard which said, 'If you want to change your writing, you must change your life.' Natalie Goldberg had a similar experience with her Zen teacher, Suzuki Roshi. She never quite seemed to 'get' what he was telling her about her meditation practice. In the end he told her that *writing* was her spiritual path. Writing was her gift and it was there that she would meet her own loneliness, her impatience, her deepest doubts and her wildest joy.

Maybe you have to change your religion, your hairstyle, your circle of friends. Maybe you have to come out of the closet, or maybe you just need to clean out your closet. Good luck with discovering all the many facets of yourself, and with exploring the unique conditions that help *you* write.

The following poem, written by me after reading Diane Ackerman's essay, shows some of the strange habits writers have. What are some of yours?

Certain Difficulties

Virginia Woolf wrote standing up.
So did Hemingway.
Edith Sitwell lay in a coffin.
George Sand made love first.
Colette picked the fleas off her cat and then
    began.
Schiller sniffed rotten apples.
D.H. Lawrence climbed naked in his mulberry tree.

Others smoked cigars,
took opium,
or wrote while soaking
in the bath.

Kurt Vonnegut ties himself to a chair.

Seems like no one finds
this writing business easy.

Exercises

✢ Write a description of your perfect writing day.

✢ What are the main blocks to your creativity?

✢ What activities make you feel better about being you?

Take a quality you'd like to have more of. Originality? Playfulness ? Courage? Can you imagine what that quality would be like if it was a person. What do they look like? What do they wear? Where do they hang out? Here's an example:

Lara Lazy-Girl has crusty food stains on her sweatshirt and a bird nesting in her smelly dreadlocks. Her best friends are Casey-Can't-Be-Bothered and Mick Maybe-Later. Lara Lazy-Girl owes $27 in overdue library fines, left her mobile phone on the train, and is still wearing last Tuesday's underpants.

Here's a couple of good quotes to encourage you to be yourself, especially if you've been told you're too sensitive, too creative, too dreamy, or too anything. Relax. Enjoy being who you are. You're a writer.

> Writing, when all's said and done, is an attempt to understand one's own circumstance and to clarify the confusion of existence, including insecurities that do not torment normal people, only chronic non-conformists, many of whom end up as writers having failed in other undertakings.   Isabel Allende

> The truly creative mind in any field is no more than this: A human creature born abnormally, inhumanly sensitive. To him...a touch is a blow, a sound is a noise, a misfortune is a tragedy, a joy is an ecstasy, a friend is a lover, a lover

is a god, and failure is death. Add to this cruelly delicate organism the overpowering necessity to create, create, create — so that without the creating of music or poetry or books or buildings or something of meaning, his very breath is cut off from him. He must create, must pour out creation. By some strange, unknown, inward urgency he is not really alive unless he is creating.

Pearl S. Buck

Sometimes it's really hard

I like writing. When everything else gets too difficult and confusing, I can retreat to my desk and play with the muddle and despair and curiosity, knit it into paragraphs.   Mari Rhydwen

A writer is someone for whom writing is more difficult than it is for other people.   Thomas Mann

Many people hear voices when no one is there. Some of them are called mad and shut up in rooms where they stare at the walls all day. Others are called writers and they do pretty much the same thing.

Margaret Chittenden

If we are not willing to fail we will never accomplish anything. All creative acts involve the risk of failure.

Madeleine L'Engle

Writing is hard. It is a journey into the wilderness of your heart. If you're serious about being a writer you will meet your own darkness, your impatience, your frustration, your sorrow and your pain. You'll also meet your joy and delight, which is a beautiful and wonderful thing. However, sometimes all the pleasure slips away. The work comes to a terrifying halt. Perhaps it's a technical problem. It may be a crisis of faith, or a dry patch in the imagination. Whatever the reason, there are times when the writing just won't come. All your good ideas are gone and all that remains is the gut-wrenching anxiety of feeling blocked. You're not alone, but knowing that won't be much help.

Somerset Maugham famously said, 'There are three rules for writing a novel. Unfortunately no one knows what they are.' Funny perhaps, yet horribly true and not very hilarious if you are a stuck writer whose aspirations have been replaced by a weary mixture of anxiety, boredom and shame, wrapped in the greasy newspaper of self-doubt. When you've lost your way you'd give anything to know what those three rules are.

Every writer has to face the perils of the creative journey. Paul Simon, for example, says it usually takes him three months to write a song, and that for him, songwriting is 'trial and error, endlessly' and he always feels he's 'in a vacuum, that nothing will come'.

Perseverance

Perseverance is a vital ingredient. Are you prepared to keep at it, even when it's utterly challenging? Sometimes you will need a huge amount of dedication just to keep going. You have to trust the process and continue trying things out, even when it feels as if you are swimming in porridge, or wobbling on a tightrope over a wild river. There are no easy answers during the hard passages, and you can feel very lost and vulnerable, muddling along, making it up as you go.

Many writers and artists have addressed the issue of being blocked. It seems there is a recognisable order of proceedings in the creative journey. In the beginning there is the aspiration. You have an idea. You begin to produce some work. It feels good. However at some point, it gets really hard. It doesn't feel like part of the creative process. It just feels like failure and stuckness. It feels like all is lost. However, if you persevere, somehow, out of the chaos and the darkness, new ideas and energies arise. The song or painting or novel emerges, fully itself in unimaginable ways.

One of the most important things to remember here is to feel free to make mistakes, as Ross Bolleter advises. Allow yourself to experiment, and relax into the creative process. This is incredibly important. A generous attitude to ourselves, even and especially in times of misery, is a great gift. Self-blame, gloom and negativity are hugely destructive to creativity.

Take new directions

Remember, a yacht doesn't make a sea voyage by travelling in a straight line. It zig zags, but it gets there safely in the end. Allow yourself to zig zag, to be illogical, to take new directions. It can be helpful to do something that feeds your spirit, such as listening to your favourite music, taking a long walk, seeing a movie, reading a book, drawing with bright colours. Sometimes the sheer act of stepping back and breathing deeply gives the subconscious permission to produce whatever is required to bring the work to completion, or at least traverse that particular tricky terrain. Trust that in its own good time, you'll come to a rich and fertile patch again, from which inspired ideas will emerge.

You have to abandon certainty, to let go. This takes courage. Trust that it is all right to not know where you are going. You only have to be prepared to take the journey for, as Albert Einstein said, 'If we knew what we were doing, it wouldn't be called research, would it?'

Despite the fact that writing can be a difficult path, the best way to counteract this is to bring pleasure into your working world. One of my favourite one-liners goes like this: 'It is important to have 10% nonsense in your life.' When I mention it to people they always take the percentage up a bit. My friend Brett says 90% works for him! So, when you hit the doldrums, take a break and have some fun. What will it take to feed your soul, and bring a sense of energy and delight to your work?

Remedies for the dark times

- Do something you love. Something that involves being creative, but in a different field from writing. Mosaics, cooking, planting flowers, sewing, collage, photography, playing a musical instrument, building, making sandcastles.

- Feed yourself with books, music, movies, galleries.

- Talk to other people about what nourishes them creatively. Ask what works for them, when their creative well runs dry. Some of the ideas may be quite odd.

- Get help with the technical stuff. Ask a teacher, a fellow writer, do some internet research, get a book about writing out from the library. Use every resource available to help you solve the problem.

What about when absolutely nothing works

* Firstly, remember that all writers hit these patches, as do musicians, actors, artists and architects. As Paul Simon says, most of the time you're walking around having temper tantrums, waiting for it. So throw away the notion that creativity is an easy road. It isn't. Get used to it!

* Give yourself the gift of tenderness. Don't punish yourself. Remember the Buddhist wisdom: *Everything changes*. If you allow it and take life gently, this hard patch will pass all by itself.

A few thoughts that might help

Best selling author John Grisham estimates he received 30 rejection letters before finding a publisher for his first novel, *A Time To Kill*.

I spent the morning putting in a comma and the afternoon taking it out.   Oscar Wilde

Laugh it up, fuzzball.   Han Solo

You have to have chaos in yourself in order to give birth to a dancing star.   Friedrich Nietzsche

Take heart. It's just part of the joy/torture/white magic/black magic/soaring/slough of despond that storytellers are born to live.   Perle Besserman

Writing's a lot like cooking. Sometimes the cake won't rise, no matter what you do, and every now and again the cake tastes better than you ever could have dreamed it would.   Neil Gaiman (*Fragile Things* 2006)

How do I work? I grope.   Albert Einstein

Extra techniques for when you're stuck

Brainstorming

Brainstorming is a great tool if you are stuck for a story idea, or stuck for a good ending, or just generally stuck. It's a technique that was originally devised for groups, but it can easily be done by an individual, and it involves setting a problem, then freely generating lots of possible solutions, without judging or analysing them. However wild, wacky, strange or bizarre an idea may be, it is welcome. This is a playful exercise designed to loosen the mind and let the left-field ideas come on in.

Mind mapping

Mind mapping is another useful tool when you're feeling blocked creatively. It involves using a diagram to represent words, ideas and items linked to and arranged radially around a central key word or idea. It's used to generate, visualise, structure and classify ideas, and as an aid to study, organisation, problem solving and decision making.

176

(If you're interested in knowing more about brainstorming and mind mapping, use your search engine. The net is a fabulous place to find out about such things.)

Do it badly

Just for a page, just for today, write badly. Write the worst you possibly can. Use clichés, flabby adjectives, unnecessary adverbs. Be redundant, verbose, and tell don't show. Have a ball with hackneyed metaphors and similes, and overworked phrases. You can have a lot of fun with this, and at the same time, purge yourself of those bad habits. Okay, Go! Get it out of your system once and for all.

Get a writing partner

If you know someone who is also into writing, use each other for feedback, encouragement and inspiration. You're much more likely to finish a piece of work if you have to take it to a meeting with your writing buddy. Make a plan to meet every Saturday at your favourite café. Set a writing topic, and each bring along what you wrote. Read them to each other and give constructive critique. Or bring writing topics and write in the café. One easy writing topic is to make up stories/histories for everyone you see there. Give them fascinating lives. Use everything you see around you as writing material.

Plundering the minds of others

When you feel blocked, ask the universe for help. Try the internet, the library, workshops; ask your teacher, ask your friends. When I was writing *Follow the Blue* I got stuck with an important plot point. Something had to go wrong at a party, because if you set up a party and everything goes right, it's boring. The most obvious thing that could go wrong would be if the party was gate-crashed. I didn't want to use a clichéd idea so I asked a whole bunch of women friends for suggestions. I heard some truly terrifying tales of things that had gone wrong at parties! However, I also was given a story that I was able to use in my book. Thank you, Zoe Thurner, for the exploding handbasin anecdote. You saved my butt.

A writing group

If you have a group of friends who like to write, start a writing group. Arrange to meet once a week, or every fortnight, or most Sundays, and be playful about the form it takes. Throw writing topics in a hat, pull one out, and all write a page on that topic. Workshop your short stories, giving each other advice and suggestions. Have creative outings, such as visiting the art gallery together, then writing in response to the piece of art that interests you the most, or write character sketches of the people you see in the gallery.

The artist's date

This idea belongs to Julia Cameron and comes from her fantastic book, *The Artist's Way*. Each week do something that will feed you creatively. It has to be something just for you, not an activity that will impress others or meet their expectations of you. It doesn't have to cost anything. It might be walking in the park, buying new art materials, getting out your favourite video, making puppets, making cards, planting flowers, visiting your grandfather, listening to jazz records. The only criteria is that whatever you choose should leave you feeling relaxed and creative.

Writing games

Games are good when you're feeling dull, stuck or bored. They provide a chance to play, have fun, enjoy, sparkle and grin. You can do them alone, in pairs or in a group. Don't underestimate the power of being silly. It can really loosen you up.

Bad Names for Boats

My husband and I invented this one during a road trip. It's designed to exercise both your imagination and your sense of humour. It's very simple. All you do is invent good bad names for boats. Here are a few of ours:

- That Sinking Feeling

- Tanglewreck

- Spew and die

- Chunderbucket

- Going Down Screaming

- Farquingnightmare

- Bottom Dweller

∂ Incredibly Rusty Heap

  ∂ Hole in the sea you throw money in

  ∂ Prison with a chance of drowning

The If Game

This one works best with at least four people, and
splendidly in a larger group. It's kind of like Consequences,
which you might have played as a kid, where each player
draws the head of a person, bird or animal, then folds the
paper so that head can't be seen, leaving only the marks
where the torso should go, and passes their paper to the
left. The next player draws a torso, and the manouevre is
repeated with legs. The resulting amalgams provide many
hours of happy fun. In the word version, the first player
writes the word If and completes a sentence, then turns
down their page so the sentence can't be seen. The paper
gets passed four times, the beginning words for each
of the four sequences are as follows:
If … I would … And … Until …

Here are some examples from the If Game:

If I were a castaway on a desert island,
I would swim hard through the water
And each time I opened my mouth a laugh
    would come out
Until the next blue moon.

If I were a banana farmer
I would have the world at my feet
And it was once upon a time like that
Until I am madly in love with a seahorse

If I were going on an exciting journey
I would fly high
And then I'd love to play the piano
Until the sun came up

If I were able to write full-time
I would be courageous and fun and beautifully
   purple
And float to the stars on wings of silver
   gossamer
Until next Saturday

Grab bag

This is a game I often play with a group of writers,
although there's no reason why you can't play it by
yourself. Fill a pouch with interesting objects such as:
a shell, a blue marble, a green peg, a broken piece of
jewellery, a plastic cowboy, a tiny photograph, a quirky
fridge magnet. Each person dips their hand in the bag, and
starts to write, responding to whatever is in the bag. There
is no such thing as a 'correct' story. The green peg may
inspire a memory about your grandmother who always
washed the clothes on Monday, or a sci-fi piece about
aliens disguised as green pegs.

Truth and lies

Great for groups and at sleepovers. Each player tells the others three things, two of which are true and one of which is a lie. The group has to guess which one is the lie.

Bragging

I love this two-person game that I found in Paul Matthews' book, *Sing Me the Creation*. Matthews is a Steiner teacher, a poet and a juggler, and the book is a fantastic collection of writing games and exercises designed to enhance and encourage the imagination. The Bragging Game is heaps of fun, and allows the part of you which needs to tell more lies and be more outrageous to play. You need two players, or sets of two players. Each pair takes a piece of paper, and two pencils. The first person writes down a statement and hands it to their partner, who has to 'top it' in some way. They then hand the paper back to the other person, who again has to 'top' the statement.

The example in the book starts with Player A stating 'Yesterday I saw a daisy crying.' That's nothing, says Player B. Yesterday I saw a rose and a tulip laughing. Quite a few brilliant exchanges later, Player A states, 'I am God.' You wouldn't think anyone could trump that, but Player B does so brilliantly, responding, 'I am your mother.'

Three word sets

Jerry Cleaver, author of *Immediate Fiction*, suggests kick-starting a dull patch by writing from three word sets. Pick any three words, strong nouns or verbs work well, but feel free to chuck in a superb adjective. You might want to do this with some writing friends.

Write good words on slips of paper and throw them in a hat or basket. Then pick three out, and use them to inspire a piece of writing. Possible sets:

- ❖ Apricot, moon, scissors

- ❖ Gypsy, mobile phone, kitten

- ❖ Elbow, dictionary, blue

- ❖ Kingdom, castle, macaroni

- ❖ Misery, rosebud, sneaker

- ❖ Alphabet, fire, hula hoop

Who does what?

This is a fun game to use in a group. It forces the players to practise the art of showing, not telling. Write various occupations on scraps of paper, or use the ones on the next page. Now write the same number of activities on slips of paper, or use the ones on page 186. Each player takes two slips of paper, then writes a paragraph of a scene which illustrates the person doing the activity, without specifically stating who it is or what they are doing. The writer then reads the passages aloud and the other people have to guess who was doing what.

The Characters:

- a Buddhist monk
- a bus driver
- a very beautiful woman
- a gardener
- a 17-year-old hairdressing apprentice
- an ageing hippie
- a 14-year-old homeless boy
- a self-righteous vegetarian
- an alien
- a librarian
- a drunk poet
- a retired doctor
- a psychiatrist
- a girl skateboarder
- a thief
- a grumpy old lady

- a bed-ridden child
- a person in a wheelchair
- a sleepy teacher
- a chubby 11-year-old boy
- a blind middle-aged woman
- a lonely housewife
- an Italian nonna (grandmother)
- a 6-year-old girl with freckles
- a failing university student
- a gay florist
- a bored yoga teacher
- a very pregnant woman
- a cranky uncle
- Oprah Winfrey

The Activities:

- writing a letter
- channel surfing
- choosing a pair of shoes
- buying an item of food
- farting in public
- making a meal
- falling asleep
- swimming
- washing their dog
- writing a poem
- going through an old photo album
- making marmalade
- waking up
- brushing their teeth
- talking to themselves
- parking a car
- fishing
- having a bath
- cutting their toenails
- vacuuming
- refusing to go home
- buying chocolate
- talking on the phone
- frying pancakes
- playing in a park
- looking for something
- stealing flowers
- missing the bus
- at the zoo
- looking at themselves in the mirror

Epilogue

Every step of the journey is the journey.   Zen saying

I wish you happy travelling on your journey into the world
of words. All you need to do is to begin. Once you take
the first step, your writing will take you to exciting places.
Relax and enjoy.

THE BEST
THINGS ABOUT

WHY BEING A WRITER IS GOOD

You get paid to tell lies and make stuff up.

You can stay home and work in your pyjamas.

You get to travel because it's research.

You get to ask nosy questions because it's research.

You get to do strange, interesting things because its research.

You can sleep till noon, work till midnight, and take time off whenever you like.

You get to act stranger than most people and its considered okay, because you're a writer.

You don't have to share, or choose a partner. You just do it all by yourself, however you want to.

You get to read a book in your study while other people are doing housework because it looks like you are writing.

On a good day, moving an adjective and choosing a noun is most enjoyable.

"Writer" looks better on a passport than "dental hygienist." (Sorry, DH's, I am sure some of you are very interesting people.)

Your peers are often weird, wild, wise, and wonderful

You can take a tea break whenever you feel like it.

AND WORST BEING A WRITER

WHY BEING A WRITER IS BAD

Sitting all by yourself in your study for hours on end is lonely.

Staring at a blank page when you can't think of even one semi-interesting idea is terrifying and lonely.

No one pays you if you don't do anything.

Even if you work very hard, if you write something that no one wants, no one pays you and you feel like rubbish.

Even if you work very hard and someone does publish what you write, you usually get very little money. (Unless you're JK Rowling, you probably won't get really rich.)

Editors ~~nibble~~ scribble all over your work and make you start all over again.

The publisher gets to choose the cover on your book and sometimes you don't like the cover. (The girl who's supposed to be Rosie on my Italian hardback cover of Guitar Highway Rose is not at all to my liking.)

If you don't look after your body you end up with all sorts of nasty physical difficulties, such as repetitive strain injury, headaches and dodecaridiculitis. (Okay, i made the last bit up.)

Getting juicy on the net

As you probably know, there are hours of happy fun to be had surfing the internet. But now you can tell your mother, when she nags you to get off the computer, that it is actually an important resource for the writer, and Brigid Lowry told you so!

As a writer, there are many ways you can use the internet.

Research

Firstly, it's a brilliant research tool. A billion useful facts are just a key-stroke away. You can find out the time in New York, the weather in Dubai, and the words of your favourite song, as well as the population of Hanoi, or the mating habits of chimpanzees, if you should happen to need them.

Email

Email is a wonderful form of creative connection. There's a story in my latest book, *Tomorrow All Will Be Beautiful*, which gives an account of the wonderful, life-sustaining relationship between me and Grace Goodfellow. Grace was fourteen when she emailed me to tell me she liked one of my books. I emailed back, and the rest, as they say, is history. We've been writing to each other for four years now. Grace is one of the most fantastic people in my life, even though we haven't actually met in person yet. With the cyber magic of email, we've shared our loves and our laughter, our tears and our tantrums. 'A True Story of Elves and Starlight' is the story of us. Check it out!

Blogs

Now to blogging. Broaden your creative landscape by reading other people's blogs, or by writing your own. A blog is a user-generated website in which entries are made in journal style and displayed in a reverse chronological order. Blogs often have a theme, such as music; however some are intimate personal writings about the life and times of the author. A typical blog combines text, images, and links to other blogs, web pages, and related sites. Primarily textual, blogs can also include photoblog, sketchblog, vlog or podcasting.

Some random wonderful websites you can visit from the comfort of your own home!

If your imagination needs a boost, try this one.
www.duirwaighgallery.com/inspiration_aknock.htm

If you want a quote on any subject in the known universe, try this:
www.wikiquote.org

Have you met Bartleby yet? It's a site that publishes the classics of literature, non fiction and classics free of charge. Includes Bartleby's Quotations, Columbia Encyclopedia, World Fact Book and much more.
www.bartleby.com

Here's the link you'll need if you do want to find out the mating habits of those raunchy chimpanzees. Wikipedia is a free on-line encyclopedia with over 1,000,000 articles plus links to thousands of websites and pictures.
www.wikipedia.org

Can't remember the difference between *effect* and *affect*? Need to know what martingale means? Then visit Your Dictionary, a comprehensive and authoritative portal for language and language related matters, with more than 1800 dictionaries and 250 languages.
www.yourdictionary.com

Keen to learn more about writing and publishing? Then this one's for you. www.teenwriting.about.com is a cool youth-focused zine. It's an offshoot of an American writer's e-zine which provides a wealth of literary information and ideas. With articles, exercises and a great online work section, there's plenty to motivate and inspire.

I love The Scriptorium, a virtual room for writers. www.thescriptorium.net In each monthly issue you'll find articles, interviews, exercises, book reviews, and more to help you become the best writer you can be. Want to hang out with some fellow writers? Try the message

board, The Writer's Block, http://com4.runboard.com/
bthewritersblock

Got a poem or a short story you'd like to submit to the net?
Then Cyberteens is for you! They accept fiction, poems,
non fiction, and photography from aspiring teen authors
around the globe. www.cyberteens.com/cr

Squills is a great monthly e-zine written for young writers.
Amongst other things, it includes book reviews, short
fiction stories, user-submitted poems and writing tips.
www.youngwriterssociety.com/squills.php

Many authors have websites. For some, you can find them
via their publisher. For example, try Allen & Unwin's
website to get author profiles and the latest titles of their
fabulous authors: www.allenandunwin.com

Some authors have their own websites:
www.pauljennings.com.au
www.johnmarsden.com.au
www.annefine.co.uk
www.terrypratchettbooks.com
www.jkrowling.com
www.tasman.net/~penwoman

Aaron Shepard is another author worth meeting. You'll
find lots of goodies on his site, including ten helpful tips
for young authors. www.aaronshep.com/youngauthor

This is the official website of comedian, Mitch Hedberg,
www.mitchhedberg.net whom I quote here and there in

this book. He was an eccentric comedian, who died at age 37 of a drug overdose. Read more about him on Wikipedia, and find more of his quotes on http://en.wikiquote.org/wiki/Mitch_Hedberg

If you've managed to write a novel, a short story collection, a picture book or a graphic novel, well done! Now all you need is a publisher. Most publishers list information on their websites about the sort of work they are looking for, and how to submit. Many won't look at work unless it comes to them via an agent. Finding an agent is a quest in itself, but again, the web is a great way to find the necessary information.

Writing organisations can also be really helpful:
The Australian Society of Authors
www.asauthors.org
The New Zealand Society of Authors:
www.authors.org.nz
Book Council of New Zealand:
www.bookcouncil.org.nz
Children's Book Council of Australia
www.cbc.org.au
The Fellowship of Australian Writers has a branch in each state. And there are writing centres in most Australian states. Just search for writing centres in Australia.

Here is a webpage full of FAQs about the writing process, and information about what happens if you get your book published. www.realkids.com/wrifaq.shtml

If you like fantasy and speculative fiction, check this one out.
www.pjballantine.net

If you feel you aren't utilising the web to its full potential,
go to your local library and talk to the research librarian.
You will learn amazing new ways to use the web for your
benefit.

Poet, Billy Collins had a neat scheme to make sure every
American school child got a poem a day. Poetry 180, is very
cool indeed. Go visit.
www.loc.gov/poetry/180/001.html

A writer friend turned me on to Wordsmith. Every day I
am sent an interesting new word, along with its meaning
and a fabulous quote.
wordsmith.org/awad/subscriber.html

Need a laugh? This is the site for world's worst writing.
www.bulwer-lytton.com

Finally, here is a page with helpful hints from over 30
authors from around the world! www.kidsonthenet.org.uk/
authors/advice/bmitchelhill.htm

Bibliography

Ackerman, Diane. 'Courting the muse.' *A Natural History of the Senses*.
New York: Random House, 1990.

Allende, Isabelle. *My Invented Country: A Memoir*.
London: Flamingo, 2003.

Barrington, Judith. *Writing the Memoir: From Truth to Art*.
Sydney: Allen & Unwin, 2000.

Beale, Fleur. *The Transformation of Minna Hargreaves*.
Auckland: Random House, 2007.

Berg, Elizabeth. *We Are All Welcome Here*.
New York: Random House, 2006.

Bernays, Ann and Pamela Painter. *What if? Writing Exercises for Fiction Writers*.
New York: Collins Reference, 1995.

Carson Levine, Gail. *Writing Magic: Creating Stories that Fly*.
New York: HarperCollins, 2006. (A fun writing guide for kids 10 and up.)

Cameron, Julia. *The Artist's Way: A Course in Discovering and Recovering Your Creative Self*.
London: Pan Books, 1995.

Cameron, Julia. *How to Avoid Making Art (Or Anything Else You Enjoy)*.
New York: Tarcher/Penguin, 2005.

Cameron, Julia. *The Vein of Gold: A Journey to your Creative Heart.*

London: Pan Books, 1996.

Chekoway, Julie, ed. *Creating Fiction.*

Ohio: Story Press, 1999.

Cisneros, Sandra. *The House on Mango Street.*

London: Bloomsbury, 1992.

Cleaver, Jerry. *Immediate Fiction: A Complete Writing Course.*

New York: St Martins Griffin, 2002.

Duras, Marguerite. *The Lover.*

London: Flamingo,1986.

Fox, John. *Poetic Medicine: The Healing Art of Poem-Making.*

New York: Putnam, 1997.

Garner, Helen. *The Children's Bach.*

Melbourne: McPhee Gribble, 1985.

Gibb, Camilla. *Sweetness in the Belly.*

London: Vintage Books, 2007.

Gillespie, Sally. *Living The Dream: A Guide to Working with Your Dreams.*

Australia: Bantam, 1996.

Goldberg, Natalie. *Wild Mind.*

London: Rider, 1995.

Goldberg, Natalie. *Writing Down the Bones.*

Boston: Shambala, 1996.

Goldsmith Woolridge, Susan. *Poemcrazy: Freeing Your Life With Words.*

New York: Three Rivers Press, 1996.

Goodfellow, Geoff. *Triggers: Turning Experiences into Poetry.*

Adelaide: Wakefield Press, 1992.

Grenville, Kate. *The Writing Book*

Sydney: Allen & Unwin, 1990.

Hodgson, Terence. *Eyes Like Butterflies: A Treasury of Similes and Metaphors from Modern Literature in English.*
New Zealand: Steele Roberts, 2003.

Jackson, Michael. *The Accidental Anthropologist: A Memoir.*
Dunedin: Longacre Press, 2006.

Kimball, Michael. *How Much of Us There Was.*
London: Harper Perennial, 2006.

Kinross Smith, Graeme. *Writer: A Working Guide for New Writers.*
Melbourne: Oxford University Press, 1992.

Klauser, Henriette Anne. *Writing on Both Sides of the Brain.*
San Francisco: Harper, 1987.

Lamott, Anne. *Bird by Bird: Some Instructions on Writing and Life.*
New York: Anchor Books, 1994.

Marsden, John. *Everything I know about Writing.*
Melbourne: Reed Books, 1993.

Mathews, Paul. *Sing me the Creation: A sourcebook for poets and teachers, and all who wish to develop the life of the imagination.*
London: Hawthorn Press, 1994.

Metzger, Deena. *Writing for Your Life.*
New York: Harper, 1992.

Moon, Janelle. *The Wise Earth Speaks to Your Spirit: 52 Ways to Find Your Soul Voice Through Journal Writing.*
Boston: Red Wheel, 2002.

Paul, Andrea. *Girlosophy: How To Write Your own Life.*
Sydney: Allen & Unwin, 2006. (A creative and inspirational guide for creating beautiful journals, scrapbooks and diaries.)

Pringle, David, ed. *The Ultimate Encyclopedia of Fantasy.*
Forward by Terry Pratchett.
London: Carlton, 2006.

Pringle, David. *Imaginary People: A Who's Who of Modern Fictional Characters.*
United Kingdom: Grafton Books, 1987.

Pringle, David. *The Ultimate Guide to Science Fiction: An A-Z Guide to S. F.*
United Kingdom: Grafton Books, 1990.

Prose, Francine. *Reading Like A Writer: A Guide for People Who Love Books and for Those Who Want to Write Them.*
New York: Harper Collins, 2006

Rainer, Tristine. *The New Diary.*
Sydney: Angus & Robertson, 1990.

Rekulak, Joseph. *The Writer's Block: 786 Ideas to Jump-start Your Imagination.*
Philadelphia: Running Press, 2001.

Rheingold, Howard. *They Have a Word for it: A Lighthearted Lexicon of Untranslatable Words and Phrases.*
Kentucky: Sarabande Books, 2000.

Trigiani, Adriana. *Home to Big Stone Gap.*
New York: Simon and Schuster, 2006.

Whitebeach, Terry. *Four New Poets* (John Bennett, Susan Hawthorne, Beate Josephi, Terry Whitebeach)
Sydney: Penguin, 1993.

Wicks, Susan. *Driving My Father.*
London: Faber and Faber, 1995.

Winterson, Jeanette. *Tanglewreck.*
London: Bloomsbury, 2006.

Williamson, Nick. *The Whole Forest.*
Christchurch: Sudden Valley Press, 2001.

Acknowledgements

Many thanks to friends and writers who so kindly let me use their work in this book.

Bridget Auchmuty-Musters, for 'Love at First Sight'. *Published in: Kapiti Poems 7 (1994), Ten (1994), Love at First Sight (1997), Fresh Fields (2001)*

Nick Williamson, for his three haiku. Published in *The Whole Forest*. Sudden Valley Press 2001. Also in New Zealand Poetry Society Anthologies.

Jaya Penelope, for 'Dancing Pants' and 'A Small Prayer'.

Mary Jaksch, for 'Little Red Car'.

Ross Bolleter, for 'Washing at Night'.

John Turner, for his haiku.

Grace Goodfellow, for lots and lots of good bits, some from her current novel.

Fleur Beale, for the lines from 'The Transformation of Minna Hargreaves'.

Jessica Le Bas, for her constant encouragement, and her thoughts on editing.

Alison Georgeson, for 'Eddie', 'Rewinding Eddie', and 'Mah-Jongg'.

Josie de Costa, for 'For Jenna'.

200

Ben Mitchell, for a quote and a good line.
Mari Rhydwen, for her good line.
Mike Jackson and Kate Duignan, for fine quotes.

Special thanks:
To Sam Field, for encouraging me by saying that this could be the book I was born to write, and for his wise editorial help regarding science fiction and fantasy.

To Paul Fraser, who puts up with my tantrums, is always kind, and deserves to go fishing more often.

Guitar Highway Rose

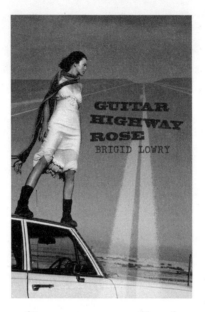

'I want to get out of here.'
'I'm coming too.'

Rosie Moon is restless. She wants to do something, be someone… be someone else. Asher is the new boy in her class. He has dreadlocks, a guitar and a case of the lonesome gypsy blues.

Some ideas are not born of logic and good sense. They sprout from nowhere and feed on excitement, sprinkled with adventure juice and the sweet flavour of the forbidden.

Part love story, part road story, Brigid Lowry's *Guitar Highway Rose* freewheels through the darker and lighter sides of life with wit, charm and compassion.

Follow the Blue

Who are you? 'Bec.'
Who are you? 'Fifteen.'
Who are you? 'Lovesick.'

First my father had his breakdown. Then my parents went away,
leaving a daggy housekeeper in their place. It was my fifteenth
summer and I was tired of being good old sensible Bec.
I wanted to be a wild and dancing kind of girl, so I dyed my hair,
discovered magic, threw my first party... and then
there was the boy thing...

Follow the Blue is a funny, touching story,
sparkling with bright summer colours.

With lots of love from Georgia

My name is Georgia.
I live in a town called Anywhere
that has too many shopping malls
and not enough skate parks.
I like to think of myself as a brilliant creative person,
but sometimes I just feel like a sad lonely girl with a big bum.

Welcome to the world of Georgia, Philosopher Queen and
list-maker extraordinaire, as she writes her way through
a bumpy year that includes part-time jobs, tricky mother stuff
and a boy with a delicious smile.